Winning in the Dojo and Your Life

Soul of the Genius Sensei

Stickman Publications, Inc.
Seattle, WA 98126

ISBN-13: 979-8-9855617-3-9

Disclaimer:
Information in this book is distributed "As Is," without warranty. Nothing in this document constitutes a legal opinion nor should any of its contents be treated as such. Neither the authors nor the publisher shall have any liability with respect to the information contained herein. Further, neither the authors nor the publisher has any control over or assume any responsibility for websites or external resources referenced in this book. When it comes to martial arts, self-defense, violence, and related topics, no text, no matter how well written, can substitute for professional, hands-on instruction. These materials should be used *for academic study only.*

Winning in the Dojo and Your Life

Soul of the Genius Sensei

Kris Wilder &
Lawrence A. Kane

Contents

INTRODUCTION

"We work to become, not to acquire."
Elbert Hubbard

The definers and shapers at the core of any society are the people in the middle, the normal work-a-day folks. No culture or organization can be driven solely by the great executive, the president, or the CEO. Sure, those at the top can craft a vision or architect a strategy, but they cannot simultaneously perform every function necessary to carry it out. To have any real shot at turning vision into reality, those in the middle must do the heavy lifting and lead.

This book was not written for the 64th floor executive. It is created for you, for us, and for others like us, the folks in the middle. We are the engine that makes society and culture what it is or what it can be. To do that, to affect people on a gut-level, to lead, we need to step into the breach where the void of leadership lies and pledge on an everyday basis that we will make others' lives better and in turn improve our own existence and the lives of our loved ones as well.

Neither author is perfect by any stretch of the imagination, yet we have done our best to learn from successes and failures alike and will do our utmost to impart our collective wisdom here. As you read through the materials try to take the same tactic. Hold up a small rearview mirror. Learn from the past, but don't dwell on your mistakes. Life is best lived forward with an eye toward the future.

We look to the title of the 1976 Broadway play by Milan Stitt, The Runner Stumbles, for a great metaphor. We are all runners in the race of life and we all stumble. It's not a matter of if, but when... The real question becomes one of whether or not we will pick ourselves back up afterward and find our stride. And, in finding our stride, will we come alongside others and encourage them as well?

Our conviction is that this book will help you do exactly that.

How to Use This Book

*"To improve is to change; to be
perfect is to change often."*

Winston Churchill

Sensei is the Japanese word for "teacher," which literally translates as "one who has come before." It's an honorific used by instructors of classical martial arts that has been adopted across a broad spectrum of society. In essence it is anyone who has acquired valuable knowledge, skills, and experience and is willing to share their expertise with others.

Clearly you cannot magically become an exemplary instructor in a mere 60-seconds any more than a businessperson can transform his or her leadership style from spending 60-seconds perusing Blanchard and Johnson's book, *The One Minute Manager.* But, you can devote a few minutes a day to honing your craft. And that's the point. It is about giving back, offering your best to others so that they can find the best in themselves. And, with appreciation, they will eventually be able pay it forward...

We've chunked this book into short, actionable chapters that most folks can read in a minute or two, hence the title. Our goal is to change the way you see the world and to arm you with knowledge and tools that will help you act on this new perspective. As you progress through the materials, look toward how you can habituate what you have learned, translating it into specific behavioral and communications goals. This will improve your relations with everyone you interact with.

In educating others, you become a role model. It's an opportunity—and a responsibility—to lead, to teach, to leave a legacy. Application, instruction, and holistic self-development, these are the hallmarks of the exceptional *sensei*. This book is designed to hone your mind and sharpen your spirit so that you can become the leader, mentor, and teacher that you were meant to be.

1. Self-Doubt and Teaching

Leveraging Constructive Feedback to Perfect your Art

"No fine work can be done without concentration and self-sacrifice and toil and doubt."
Max Beerbohm

Teaching something as serious as a fighting art carries a heavy burden of responsibility at any level, but even more so if you're the head instructor of your own school. Just like any other leader the proverbial buck stops with you. You are not only responsible for the vitality and viability of your business, but also for the safety and wellbeing of your students and fellow instructors. In fact, if you are teaching martial arts in any capacity, you have undoubtedly jumped through a myriad of multicolored flaming hoops to get where you are today... To begin you have gained enough skill and experience on the mat that somebody above you decided that you made the cut, that you are good enough to teach the basics, lead a class as part of their team, or move out and start a school on your own.

You may have found a practice space or created one, acquired or built training equipment, designed a curriculum, and set out to pass along what you have learned to others. You are likely marketing your business, billing students, paying taxes, buying insurance, balancing your bank account, and leading most every class. You're undoubtedly dealing with a host of problems too, everything from ego clashes to equipment failures, unrealistic student expectations, bad debt collections, bullying behaviors, meddlesome parents, permitting and other regulations, fire inspections, and a whole lot more... And, while you may have mastered your martial art or at least progressed a heck of a lot farther than your students, you're undoubtedly not an expert in everything that you are required to do in order to be successful. This is where self-doubt can creep in.

Self-doubt is normal, that niggling feeling that no matter how capable you are you really do not know enough, aren't good enough. It can even bring on full-blown panic attacks. Comedian Norm MacDonald once talked about his panic attack prior to a skit on the television show *Saturday Night Live*. A master of his art, veteran of uncountable nightclub performances before unpredictable crowds, he nevertheless had a panic attack so severe that he almost had to leave the show. It happens to all of us at one point or another, but successful leaders don't let self-doubt crush their dreams.

Dojo Wisdom:

> Many students join a *dojo* with the dream of earning their black belt, yet only two or three percent of those who set out to do so actually succeed. Numerous practitioners want to teach martial arts, but few are able to turn that dream into a reality. You may have a long way yet to travel on your journey, but as an active *sensei* you have already achieved an unprecedented level of success. Own it and hone it.

Action:

Are you worried that you're missing the mark, falling short of expectations? Here is a simple way to know for sure: Do a class evaluation. Make a short survey that asks the questions that will help you better understand your class and your performance and give it to your students (and their parents if you teach kids). Include inquiries about class start/stop times and durations, subject matter, rankings, focus areas, seminar subjects, teaching style, and the like. Make it blind, either via a web survey tool or by giving respondents an unmarked envelope to put it in so that anyone who wishes to remain anonymous can be.

Take these survey results seriously. They will help both you and your business grow. You will likely find that you are doing okay, and you will simultaneously discover a place or two where you can hone the edges of your teaching and improve your class.

Honing the Blade:

> No one is perfect, yet the relentless pursuit of perfection can drive an ordinary person to extraordinary heights. A challenge is that we tend to be blind to aspects of our nature that may be holding us back. That's why constructive feedback is so important. Those around us are able to see and articulate what we cannot. Embrace feedback, learn from it, and grow.

2. Creating Leaders

Seven Essentials of Leadership

"If your actions inspire others to dream more, learn more, do more and become more, you are a leader."
John Quincy Adams

Martial artists might study an art in order to learn how to fight, but we all know that *budo* (martial arts) encompasses a whole lot more than fighting. And, we know that most students who begin the journey will eventually drop out. Physical skills fade with time, but character endures. That's why leadership is as important an ingredient of exemplary martial arts instruction as any fighting technique or martial application.

Let's face it, with good situational awareness and self-restraint practitioners might never find themselves in a real fight, but in virtually every aspect of their lives they will find opportunities to lead. Leadership can stem from authority, expertise, or example. With the exception of hierarchical authority, being placed in charge, any example that others want to emulate is leadership.

While styles vary greatly, traits of good leadership consistently apply to everyone. Leveraging natural charisma is valuable, of course, but it is far less important than behaviors that demonstrate character. Without good character, people will not follow a leader over the long run. The seven essential attributes of leadership include being (1) Consistent, (2) Visionary, (3) Fair, (4) Honest, (5) Courageous, (6) Inspirational, and (7) Productive. Let's elaborate:

1. **Consistent**: earns trust and respect through integrity and dependability. Subordinates, peers, and superiors all know what to expect when interacting with this person. Reliably meets commitments.

2. **Visionary**: conveys a sense of purpose that motivates others. Able to define a strategic direction and success criteria, balance big-picture concerns with day-to-day issues, set priorities, and continuously course-correct as necessary to achieve results.

3. **Fair**: open-minded. Treats people impartially and objectively. Creates an atmosphere where folks feel comfortable bringing up problems, taking measured risks, and suggesting innovative alternatives.

4. **Honest**: means what they say and says what they mean. Keeps confidences, models integrity, and bounds pursuit of individual objectives with the overall interests of the organization or team.

5. **Courageous**: models confidence. Sees changes as opportunities and demonstrates a willingness to do the right things even when they are not expedient or politically easy.

6. **Inspirational**: builds teams whose performance is greater than the sum of their parts. Celebrates successes and learns from failures, leverages diversity, and sets people up for success.

7. **Productive**: keeps promises and delivers results. Capitalizes on unanticipated opportunities and changing circumstances to meet commitments despite challenges. Continuously improves quality and performance.

Be aware of people in your sphere of influence who set a good example by consistently demonstrating these seven leadership attributes. These individuals show up on time, work diligently, perform well, help others, and are a real asset to your school and community. Every reasonable effort should be exerted to motivate, train, and retain them. To create leaders, you need to help folks acquire the knowledge, skills, and ability for success, and give them a chance to lead. Perhaps this begins with something as simple as leading warm up exercises or some other minor aspect of the class, but it can easily build to something greater like leading a seminar, demonstration, community service project, or publishing a book on your art.

Personal development is a cycle. For example, a new rank might come with new challenges, which in turn leads to new accomplishments and ever escalating responsibility. Success breeds success, and success is a juice of its own. Your role as a *sensei* is to talk about that future with your students. Get them excited. Share your vision such as what the next rank or step will mean, and do so in concrete terms. There must be actionable items, real successes within reach, and you must give each person the right tools to have a legitimate chance at achieving them.

The formula for future talk is: **Today + Positive Action = Success** *(e.g., skill, position, title, or role, and everything that comes with it).*

This may seem to be a simple equation, but it is very powerful. People tend to act in their own enlightened self-interest, yet a common challenge is that we do not always know what our self-interest truly is or what steps are necessary to further our aspirations. That is the power of having a teacher, coach, mentor, or role model, someone who can point the way. As a *sensei* you have been there before, so you can lay out the steps, show the possibilities, explain the rewards, and help others latch onto the actions necessary to carry them out.

It's not only your job, it's your responsibility.

Dojo Wisdom:

> To create leaders, you need to help those around you acquire the knowledge, skills, and abilities they need for success. And then you need to give them a chance to put those attributes into practice. Find individuals who demonstrate the seven leadership characteristics, give them the tools they need, and a chance to lead.

Action:

You likely already know who your star pupil is, but what about the rest of your students or fellow instructors? Don't overlook the quiet folks, the ones who work hard but avoid the spotlight. Are there unsung heroes in your group who just need that one opportunity to shine?

One way to find out is to build a simple two-axis table showing "leadership potential" on one axis and "experience" on the other, using a scale of 1 (low) to 5 (high). Plot the names of everyone in your charge on that page. You can develop discrete criteria for each rating, but a subjective "gut check" placement should prove illuminating. At a glance you can identify future leaders who need your support and make sure that you haven't overlooked anyone.

Once complete, choose someone with high leadership potential who has not had a chance to grow their skills recently and find a project that is both a learning experience and an opportunity to make a real difference. Integrate this into your routine so that it becomes a continuous process and you will be amazed and pleased by the results.

Honing the Blade:

> Most people grow into challenges. They will step up or down to your expectations. As a college intern Kane was tasked with staffing two restaurants for the Seattle Sheraton hotel, a daunting task for someone with book learning and no practical experience, yet his manager set high expectations, provided resources, and got out of the way. By the end of his tenure, 239 of the 240 people Kane recommended were hired and all performed well on the job. It's not Kane's performance that was exceptional, but rather the way in which his manager Doug set him up for success. Just because someone is inexperienced does not mean that they should only be allowed to perform entry-level work.

3. Esprit De Corps

Four Keys to Group Unanimity

"Talent wins games, but teamwork and intelligence wins championships."
Michael Jordan

Most commercially successful martial arts schools are run by a group rather than by a single practitioner. This means that success or failure of the organization depends on the collective efforts of individual instructors, all of whom must be moving toward the same goals, operating as one team.

Esprit de corps is a French phrase that refers to the "spirit" of the "group," that is a sense of unity around common interests and responsibilities. In other words it is about a collection of individuals who truly collaborate. Together they hold tightly to the common goal that has been set before them such as building a program, securing a victory, or winning a championship. They believe in a collective vision so strongly that they are willing to sacrifice, subordinating their individual desires for the team and the goal.

There are four key ingredients to building esprit de corps:

1. Leadership

2. Will

3. Deference

4. Self-Discipline

The leader must have authority, granted from both above and below, and the group being led must have the will, deference, and self-discipline to carry out their leader's vision. We will explore each of these elements in detail…

1. Leadership

Power and authority are granted from both above and below. For example, General Dwight Eisenhower became supreme commander of the allied invasion of Normandy during World War II because both United States President Roosevelt and British Prime Minister Churchill said so. Nevertheless, being in charge is not enough. Eisenhower also held the hearts and minds of his subordinates, so they were willing to implement his strategy even knowing that it could cost them their lives or well-being.

If power is given from above but the troops are not on board, leadership has been lost. Conversely if a leader is beloved by his or her team but the bosses will not listen, he or she cannot acquire the resources and backing necessary to be effective. Lose both, and… well let's just say that tends to not end well. Without unity of purpose there can be no victory on the field, on the mat, or in hearts of your students or team members. Lose the authority from above and you cannot have success. Both are needed for the esprit de corps.

2. Will

The will to do what it takes to achieve, say earn a black belt, is based on desire. Desire is a powerful word. When a person says they desire something, they are speaking from the heart. The heart is not rational. Emotions that come from the heart such as love or hate are never rational. These passions make little sense to the intellect, yet they profoundly affect behavior. Another way of saying it is that desires of the heart are non-negotiable. If a person wants something bad enough it is rare that they will not find some way to achieve it even when facing significant obstacles.

In self-defense situations, for example, most confrontations end by breaking the adversary's will, not by rendering him (or her) physically incapable of continuing to fight. Similarly, the team with the most heart in the game often wins despite any disparity of talent. Even in warfare, overcoming another nation's determination to persevere assures victory, not destroying all their resources and killing all of their people. This is why willpower is so important, vital to virtually any endeavor.

3. Deference

Most martial arts are taught in a hierarchical structure, with lower ranks deferring not only to those with higher skill and experience but also to the goals and objectives of the organization. When learning potentially lethal techniques or weapons, students must follow instructions or chaos reigns and folks get needlessly hurt or killed. The challenge is that obedience is always best given rather than demanded.

For example, many students only attend public schools in the United States because it is mandated by law. They have to be at school, but they don't have to actively participate. Administrators and teachers recognize this fact and allow for self-segregation. Some students, those who truly want to learn and have the ability to handle the materials, find themselves in Advanced Placement or honors classes, while others choose to not participate in such programs. As incongruent as it may sound at first blush, a student must first have the will to be obedient to the vision that the education system is espousing before he or she can learn anything.

To clarify, deference is not subservience, but it does require subordinating one's ambitions to further the organization's cause. That is much easier for most people to do when they believe that in making the team or organization successful their individual goals will also be accomplished along the way.

4. Self-Discipline

Anyone who has tried to lose weight knows how hard it can be to stick to a plan, even when you know it is the right thing to do. It's not just a matter of willpower, but also of self-discipline. Desire comes from the heart, while discipline comes from the head. The combination of the two can lead you to great things. Self-discipline manifests in time management, diligence, and other factors necessary to stay on track and accomplish your goals.

Dojo Wisdom:

> When you dive down deep into the esprit de corps, it is like looking at an atom. If all the parts are in place—say one hydrogen atom and two oxygen atoms (H_2O)—then you get the desired output, which in this example is water. Change the equation to one hydrogen atom and one oxygen atom and the molecule becomes unbalanced. It will seek stability by acquiring another oxygen atom. Similarly, people who lack one of the three essential elements, will, deference, or self-discipline, are unstable. It is difficult to find balance when one of the three legs of the stool is lacking. While self-directed people will find this missing element on their own, others need to have it shown to them. The ability to find the gap, explain the need, and show others the way can make you a great teacher.

Action:

Pay close attention to your team, assuring that all four elements of esprit de corps are in place. Leadership is your responsibility, whereas will, deference, and self-discipline must come from your students.

As Lou Holtz, the famous Notre Dame Football coach once said, "Not everybody can be first team, but you can always put the team first." Keeping your organization's culture and expectations in mind, consider a methodical approach to team-building beyond the *dojo* such as a leadership retreat, potluck, ropes course, paintball game, or the like to bring folks closer together and channel energy in a positive direction. The activity itself is far less important than the structure it provides.

Honing the Blade:

> Most leaders understand that it is their responsibility to support their students' growth and development. Oftentimes, however, martial arts instructors are reluctant to let their students work with others outside their system or school. Nevertheless, exposure to different teaching methods, styles, and experiences often makes for better practitioners. Sending folks to seminars taught by others often helps interject a fresh approach into your organization too. Don't be insular.

4. Integrity of Teaching

Four Elements of Building and Maintaining Trust

*"Put more trust in nobility of
character than in any oath."*

Solon

Trust is rare these days. We often look back on history and longingly evoke an era of assuredness, a time when a man's word was his bond, yet this is a distorted view of what actually occurred. For example, do you know what the phrase, "Buying a pig in a poke" means? It is an expression that originated during medieval times which refers to buying a piglet in a sack by simply poking it and feeling it squirm rather than by opening up the bag and looking inside to confirm that it in fact holds a piglet and not a puppy, kitten, or rat.

Trust is not only rare, it's fragile too. Once broken it takes an enormous effort to repair, if that is even possible. Depending on the breach it may never be. There are four basic elements to trust:

1. **Purpose**: resolution to move towards a worthwhile goal.

2. **Truthfulness**: willingness to communicate what is truly happening.

3. **Ability**: capability to do or teach what a person has espoused.

4. **Results**: achieving the established goal.

Let's jump straight to number three, ability. Ability is almost always the first item a student looks to his or her instructor for, just as it is often the first measure of an instructor for themselves. Ability is important, of course, but it is not the first element of trust. The first element of trust is purpose, and a good purpose has integrity. It focuses on a valuable goal. If we teach civilian students how to perform sentry removal or assassination, for instance, it may be an entertaining exercise but is it furthering a worthwhile goal? Is that something we'd really like to see our students implement in their everyday lives?

Now these four elements of trust are not static. Situations and context can move the lines of what is most important at any given point in time, yet in most circumstances ability hovers near the bottom of the list. We need to pay more attention to purpose, truthfulness, and results. For example, Vince Lombardi played football, but his legacy endures not because of what he did on the field, but rather how he brought others to the field and got the best out of them as a coach. That's why the Super Bowl trophy is named after him.

Virtually every martial style comes with a set of rules and expectations, a code of acceptable behaviors, most of which demand that practitioners step up to a higher level than ordinary citizens who do not practice these dangerous arts. Those who live up to those expectations are held in high regard. That is where we as instructors must live if we wish to set a good example for and gain trust from our students and fellow teachers. Without trust, the other aspects of leadership and teaching are lost.

Dojo Wisdom:

> Teaching martial arts is a serious business. Instructors must balance the somber reality that they are responsible for ensuring the safety of practitioners who learn potentially deadly techniques with the truism that if classes are not enjoyable and productive no one will participate. Martial artists are in a unique position to serve as role models for their students whether they intend to or not. Consequently, etiquette and tradition become essential aspects of *budo* training, for without them we would practice nothing more than base violence.

Action:

Character is important. Students approach martial arts for a plethora of reasons, some good, some bad, and many in-between. Because we teach dangerous if not deadly techniques, the way in which students expect to use them is very important. We would like to believe that no one wants to be responsible for teaching some hothead what he or she needs to know to kill or maim another person in a drunken brawl. Consequently it's vital to create and enforce rules of behavior in our schools.

In traditional systems *dojo kun* (virtues) are recited either at the opening or closing of class. Students and teachers alike recite the *kun* in hopes of making all those attending better people, both physically and mentally. This ritual is meant to instill a positive ideal in each person hearing it. That level of formality may or may not be appropriate in your individual circumstances, but clearly articulating expected behaviors during class and on your website is very good thing. It can protect your reputation and livelihood too.

If you haven't already created and communicated a set of precepts for your school, do it now. Once created, be certain that they are actually followed.

Honing the Blade:

> The more respected you are the less you have to say
> or do to get others to follow your example. This is, of
> course, a double-edged sword as any parent whose
> kindergartner has dropped an F-bomb in class well
> knows. Be conscious and conscientious in what you
> do.

5. Team Dynamics

Five Stages of Organizational Evolution

*"I was a captain of both my high school and
college football teams. On my high school team,
we had a 2–7 record. My college team went
9–0. Each team had great players, yet there
was a major difference in the results. The 9–0
team put the team goals ahead of individual
goals. We knew that if we put the success of the
team first, the individual goals would come."*

David Schmidt

New teams virtually never mesh instantly, even when comprised of seasoned professionals. For example, when a student earns his or her black belt and is asked to take on more of a teaching role they often struggle with transition. This new position requires thoughts and actions that can be significantly different from what they had grown accustomed to during the roughly four to eight years (depending on the system and the individual) that most folks take to earn their *shodan* or equivalent rank.

Teams tend to go through a phased cycle, something that psychologist Bruce Tuckman first postulated in 1965 as (1) forming, (2) storming, (3) norming, and (4) performing. This process not only works for a new team, but also for existing ones where new members are introduced into the mix, something that happens all the time in martial arts schools. Many folks add a fifth stage, "mourning," to Tuckman's list to include the point where a work team is disbanded at the end of a project or where a significant change in membership takes place.

The five phases of teaming work as follows:

1. **Forming**: members are brought together and tasked with an assignment to accomplish. The forming stage is usually short in duration, but includes the process of members getting to know each other and figuring out who is responsible for what aspect of the effort.

2. **Storming**: members' emotions often come into play as they clarify the team's goals and objectives, jockey for position within the roles, and collectively reach commitment about what will be done.

3. **Norming**: once team members have gotten to know each other better and feel comfortable with their assignments, they can formulate how best to work together to reach the superiorordinate goal the team was created to achieve. There is often a prolonged overlap between storming and norming phases.

4. **Performing**: the group culture is strong enough that all individuals function effectively as a single team, even when challenges or interpersonal conflicts arise.

5. **Mourning**: most teams disband at some point due to successful completion of the project, culmination of the deployment, organizational

realignment, reassignment of priorities, folks moving on to other things, or an end of the season.

A challenge of the storming and norming phases, particularly the latter, is the need for members to establish a hierarchy and cement their positions within the team. Consider situations where parents and children train together yet where the younger person outranks their older one or situations where someone is promoted into a teaching role and leads a class for former peers for a common martial arts example of this.

Pay close attention to how new members are integrated into your team. There are good and bad ways for leaders to understand each other's capabilities and develop mutual respect. As new instructors join or leave your team as well as when students come and go from class it is important to be conscious of how these changes are handled. A little formality can go a long way toward assuring consistent, smooth transitions.

Dojo Wisdom:

> One of the healthier martial traditions is bowing to (or saluting in some way) one's training partners before and after practicing together. It's not only a sign of respect, but also recognition that there is something to be learned from everyone who is willing to share, no matter what their rank. In helping others achieve we improve ourselves too.

Action:

Just as successful businesses script every phase of their new employee onboarding process, from before they begin their job, through their probation period, to the successful completion of their first year, martial arts instructors should create and follow an onboarding process for new students and teachers. It doesn't have to be complicated; a simple checklist will suffice in many circumstances so that you won't forget anything important. A student handbook or website that explains the system, style, and expectations is very useful too.

The details may vary, but the focus of this process should be on creating a welcoming atmosphere and providing the guidance necessary for folks to be successfully integrated into your club and culture. Paying attention to team dynamics will help you build and sustain an intentional culture and productive spirit for your organization.

Honing the Blade:

> As you know, *sensei* in Japanese translates as "teacher," but it also means "one who has gone before." As a *sensei* you're neither all-knowing nor all-powerful, but you do have valuable experience that others seek. Don't let them struggle. There is immense satisfaction that can be gained in seeing your students easily pick up what you had to learn the hard way due to your coaching and guidance. Keep standards high, but challenge yourself to make it easier to learn from you than it was for you to learn from your instructor(s).

6. Problems are Normal

Six Ways to Instantly Improve Problem Solving

"Good management is the art of making problems so interesting and their solutions so constructive that everyone wants to get to work and deal with them."

Paul Hawken

During his storied career Al Davis, owner of the NFL's Oakland Raiders, was a head coach, general manager, and league commissioner. He helped form both the American Football League and the National Football League. His Oakland Raiders won the Super Bowl three times. No small achievements, these accomplishments were driven by hard work and skill. You see, successful people like Davis do not assume that all is going to go according to plan. That means that they put good people in place and trust their team to make good choices, yet they also know people are human and things can go sideways if not monitored.

This realization that problems are normal is not an acceptance, a willingness to let things go off course; it is simply a fact. The natural state of the world is not convergence, it is about entropy, the degradation of systems. Every system, be it a sports team, a business, a university, or a martial arts school has to be fed energy in order to stave off the ever-present entropy. Problems can fall into two basic groups: external and internal. External problems are obstacles that come from outside of a system, in this case outside your body. Internal problems are the ones that you experience within yourself. We will be going into more depth in regard to those issues in the chapter where we discuss <u>flawed thinking</u>, so we will stick to dealing with external problems here.

When somebody comes to you with a problem, there are six essential elements you need in order to successfully assist them. These include (1) Setting a time limit, (2) Being a reporter, (3) Leveraging the angels of the angles for good communication, (4) Expressing empathy, (5) Understanding their agenda, and (6) Using thoughtful speech. Let's elaborate…

1. Set a time limit

How big is your organization? A mere twenty minutes apiece times ten people and you've taken up nearly half your day without doing anything other than listening to problems. No matter how deeply you care, no matter how empathetic you are, no matter how much time you have available, it will never be enough if you do not set limits. Part of empathy is assuring that your folks know that you will be there for them when they need you. That is good. In certain instances, you need to drop everything and listen to a friend, family member, or team member's problem. But, make sure that you manage your time effectively or you will never get anything else done.

2. Be a reporter

Good reporters need to understand facts, the Who, What, Where, When, Why, and How (5 Ws and an H). These are the basic elements necessary to figure out what has occurred and present the evidence in a clear, informative manner. If a person comes to you with an issue, you need to understand what is going on before you can offer up meaningful advice.

It is often difficult for people under emotional duress to effectively communicate the five elements that are needed for you to make an informed decision, so it's important to exercise active listening. In this fashion you will become meaningfully engaged and avoid jumping to conclusions. The basics of active listening include:

- **Paying attention**: look at the person talking. Let them see you looking at them. Do not glance at the clock or your watch. Do not start typing on your keyboard, texting on your smartphone, or looking out the window. Shut down your own mind and listen all the way through. Then pause and think about it. A pause before answering can also work as a "pattern interrupt." Because you are obviously thinking and listening, the other person must slow down to figure out what is going on. That forces them to stop counting on their own mental scripts and become fully engaged as well.

- **Asking open-ended questions**: remember that this is about gathering the 5 Ws and an H. You want to ask questions that cannot be answered with one word. "Did you get into an argument with Sarah?" is closed. "What happened when you and Sarah interacted early today?" is open. The latter encourages a story. You don't just learn from the narrative of events, you also learn about the other person by what he or she emphasizes or leaves out, what makes them excited or subdued.

- **Concentrate on emotion and demeanor**: when the words say one thing and the emotion says another, bet on emotion for true motive.

Pay attention to your own emotions too, not just to those of the person communicating with you. Sometimes there are hints, subtleties your subconscious noticed that have not yet made it to your conscious brain. If you find yourself getting agitated, angry, or anxious pause for a moment and figure out why.

- **Use paraphrasing to demonstrate understanding**: double-check your understanding by repeating back the other person's key points in your own words. "Let me see if I got this right..." It is good to clear up any miscommunication early. This may also be the time to point out body language or incongruities that make you doubt the other person's words where appropriate. You can get huge amounts of information when people try to clarify, especially when they are trying to explain away obvious emotion while struggling to seem calm.

3. Leverage the angels of the angles for good communication

There's an old kindergarten song that is sung by almost every child at one time or another. The little song is easy to remember because the title of it is *Head, Shoulders, Knees, and Toes*. This song is not just for kids, however; it is a key to body language that you can use to open the lines of communication with whomever you are talking with.

- **Head**: head position communicates an enormous amount of information. Turned slightly sideways looking with one eye denotes suspicion. Holding your chin too high indicates a position of superiority making it difficult for somebody in a subordinate position to communicate. Looking down over the top of your glasses... that equals condescension. The best head technique to get more information out of another person is a simple nod, up and down for yes. Yes, I hear you, yes, I understand you, and yes that makes sense.

- **Shoulders**: proxemics comes into play here. Standing directly in front of someone who is not a close friend or family member with your shoulders squared to them will result in a lizard-brain response. What we mean by lizard brain is that they will immediately dive into "fight, flight, or freeze" mode. It is difficult for a person to engage the cognitive aspects of their upper brain when their hindbrain is telling them that it is fight-or-flight time. To avoid this reaction, stand like people do at bars or other social events, with the shoulders at an angle.

- **Knees and toes**: pointing the foot in the direction of what you are trying to explain is a subtle technique that allows for you to focus the other person's attention toward the subject at hand. For instance, a coach discussing a defensive back's behavior to a wide receiver can point his toe in the direction of the occurrence setting attention to that moment. It allows them to discuss something that happened in the past in very real terms by focusing the athlete's mind on exactly what occurred. The student can replay the moment, understanding the complexity of what took place with little interference from the lizard brain.

4. Express empathy

"I understand."

The simple phrase "I understand" is a great opener once you have established the 5 Ws and an H. We also suggest adding the aforementioned head nod and then repeat the problem back to the person you are speaking with in your own words. Oftentimes, sharing a personal experience that helps demonstrate the fact that you truly do understand. The cool thing about empathy is that most decent people already have it in spades, though most don't express it naturally. That's where active listening comes in, it simultaneously assures that you understand the situation and are able to make the other person feel like you care enough to help them find a way to resolve it.

5. Understand their agenda

When somebody brings you a problem the first thing you need to do is uncover their agenda. When you boil it down, there are really only two choices: (1) to escape responsibility or (2) to grow into the responsibility. Your job is to find out which one of these two paths the person is trying to exercise and deal with it accordingly. While it may seem that others should always grow into the responsibility that is not always practicable, particularly when timeframes are short. You've probably heard the term "upward delegation." More often than not it's an attempt to dodge responsibility, but sometimes it really is appropriate. Leaders help break down roadblocks, acquire resources, and resolve problems, but they cannot and should not do everything themselves.

6. Use thoughtful speech

When you are approached with a problem you will often need to slow down the rate at which you speak. Slow speech with pauses demonstrates thoughtfulness and care. It is a natural output of active listening. Further, slowing things down (within reason) tends to make the communication special. One simple technique for doing this is to silently count to three before responding to the other person. You may have already constructed your mental response, but the pause demonstrates thoughtfulness, that their issue has real meaning to you. And it assures that they've truly finished speaking. Once you have that connection you can begin successful communication. Further, slowing things down when you can allow for deeper thought.

The way other people read your emotion and intent is through the rate, tone, pitch and volume of your voice. Rate and volume are indicators of intensity, whereas tone and pitch indicate the quality of emotion. The more excited someone is, whether anger or fear or even love, the louder they tend to be. And the faster they talk. This is part of why speaking slowly can denote wisdom as long as you don't overdo it.

Dojo Wisdom:

> Problems are problems. They are normal and expected, so much so that if everything went according to plan you would probably have nothing to do. Embrace these challenges as opportunities to make things better for yourself and your team.

Action:

When somebody comes to you with a problem, make sure that they are actually asking for help rather than venting or otherwise getting something off their chest. If so, use the problem-solving structure to set a time limit, be a reporter, utilize the right body language for good communication, express empathy, understand their agenda, and employ thoughtful speech. In this fashion you can come up with well-reasoned solutions while simultaneously building rapport with your team.

Honing the Blade:

People generally prefer to avoid conflict, so it takes guts for someone to come to you with a problem, particularly when they think you might be the cause of their dilemma. More so if they are subordinate to you in rank, experience, or age. While it is easy to be offended, do your best not to take such things personally. Keep your responses professional. It is easier to do so when you consider that a hallmark of good leadership is the fact that your team member found you approachable enough to express their concern in the first place.

7. Exemplary Students

Separating the Wheat from the Chaff

"It takes more than a flash of cash and sporadic attendance to succeed in a traditional dojo. Students must be considered worthy and dedicated by their instructor. More is expected of a martial artist than an ordinary person."

Dave Lowry

Nowadays just about anyone can pay an initiation fee, buy a uniform, and join almost any martial arts studio in the country. While many do just that, in a pattern reminiscent of health club memberships an awful lot of them drop out within the first few months. In the old days, on the other hand, training was more than simply attending lessons and picking up new skills. *Budoka* were part of a privileged group who tended to follow a life-long path toward becoming better people as well as highly skilled practitioners. Candidates had to earn the right to train rather than merely showing up with money to get started. Schools in feudal Japan, for instance, were extraordinarily selective. Gaining admission was an onerous process that weeded out all but the most devoted acolytes.

Turnover rates among students being what they are nowadays, few instructors devote their full attention to new practitioners until they have proven that they are worthy of such training over a period of time. As an experienced martial arts instructor, it is easy to become jaded, overlooking exceptional students who deserve your full attention. The rare person who demonstrates discipline, perseverance, and a positive attitude is an asset to both their school and their art form, and should be treated accordingly.

Characteristics of an exemplary student include the following:

1. **Good character**: a high degree of integrity, personal honor, and strong moral rectitude.

2. **Inquisitiveness**: willingness to ask questions and admit what they don't know.

3. **Passion**: enthusiasm to actively participate and learn.

4. **Respectability**: a sense of propriety and good manners, both inside and outside the *dojo*.

5. **Focus**: a sense of harmony and balance amongst their priorities.

6. **Diligence**: a strong work ethic.

7. **Perseverance**: ability to push through adversity in order to meet goals.

8. **Open mindedness**: a desire to learn form and share knowledge with others.

Students who demonstrate these eight attributes are a real asset to their class. Every reasonable effort should be exerted to motivate and retain them. While all students are worthy of and entitled to the best instruction possible, placing extra emphasis on recognizing and nurturing exemplary students has benefits that extend beyond the individual to serve as an example to which all members of a *dojo* can aspire. Special attention directed toward these individuals can raise the level to which every student aspires and ultimately achieves.

Dojo Wisdom:

> You can tell a lot about how a school is run by looking across the *dojo* floor during class. Take a moment to view your school through the eyes of a visitor from time to time and reflect upon what you see. Is the place neat, orderly, and in good repair? Is there adequate room to train? Are students standing around looking confused or does everyone appear to be actively engaged in the learning process? Are they talking or practicing? Is there an appropriate emphasis on safety? Do students and teachers interact in a respectful manner? Is attendance strong?

Action:

When you recognize exemplary students, do a little extra to encourage and support them. This might include a one-on-one coaching session, seminar invitation, membership on a demonstration or competition team, a chance to teach others, or a similar reward that is appropriate to the individual. Whatever you choose, it is important to communicate that the opportunity was earned through hard work and perseverance or it may be taken as a sign of favoritism which will backfire.

Honing the Blade:

> Balance between one's personal and professional life is important. While daily training is an admirable quality, it should not be done at the expense of family, friends, school, or business commitments. Martial arts are only sustainable over the long run when practice fits harmoniously within a larger set of life priorities.

8. Flawed Thinking

Fifteen Negative Attitudes to Banish from Your Brain

"It's fine to celebrate success but it is more important to heed the lessons of failure."

Bill Gates

Kane has interviewed and hired hundreds of people. When he was first assigned that responsibility a quarter century ago, he was required to take a course on rater errors to become a better hiring manager. Our goal in this section is similar to that rater errors class, helping you become aware of preconceived notions that may distort your thinking in unproductive ways so that you can minimize if not eliminate their impact.

Distorted thinking tends to bring negative thoughts to the forefront, inhibiting performance and achievement. Left unaddressed it can become a self-fulfilling prophecy which is detrimental for you or any member of your team who gets caught up in this behavior. The various types of distorted thinking we discuss here are adapted from the work of psychologists McKay, Davis, and Fanning. The original concept was published in 1981 in their book *Thoughts & Feelings*. It is a great resource that can help address anxiety, frustration, and many other negative emotions using cognitive therapy techniques.

The fifteen distortions include: (1) Filtering, (2) Polarized Thinking, (3) Overgeneralization, (4) Mindreading, (5) Catastrophizing, (6) Personalization, (7) External Control, (8) Internal Control, (9) Fairness, (10) Blaming, (11) Must, (12) Emotional Reasoning, (13) Resisting Change, (14) Being Right, and (15) Heaven's Reward. We will briefly explain each distortion, provide our recommendations for overcoming it, and then give you some "homework," a task of the week.

This is a long chapter which will take a whole lot more than a couple minutes to read, so you should chunk it into 15 small sections to make it more approachable. In fact, if you accept our challenge and tackle one of these tasks each week over the next fifteen weeks you will notice a marked change in your thinking. Like rater error interview training it will not make you a different person, but it will make you keenly aware of what you may have been unconsciously doing and kick-start a change in your perception.

1. Filtering

"Exaggeration is truth that has lost its temper."

Khalil Gibran

Filtering is when you take details and magnify them to the extreme, distorting actual events. A single element is picked out and the whole event becomes colored by this facet. Much like spending a wonderful evening on a date only to focus on the parking ticket you received while you were dining, when you pull negative things out of context, isolated from all the good experiences around you, you make them larger and more awful than they truly are. This can result in biased or prejudicial thinking when focused externally on others, or in becoming sad or depressed if focused internally on yourself.

We recommend:

When a negative event takes place put it into context. For example, Kane recently forgot to lock his truck. Someone rifled through the contents and stole all the change out of his ashtray (it's an old truck). While he was upset at losing a few bucks, he felt fortunate that the vehicle was undamaged and took it as a lesson to keep things secured rather than a statement on the inherent untrustworthiness of humanity. A vandalized vehicle, stolen radio, slashed tire, or the like would have been a much bigger inconvenience, harder to replace than a few bucks in pocket change.

Task of the week:

For the next week avoid using extreme words such as, "always," "never," "every time," and "all the time." These words can oftentimes be construed as accusatory. For example, "You always do XY&Z." We've all said that, yet we also know that nobody always does something, every time, all the time.

2. Polarized Thinking

"Morals are private. Decency is public."

Rita Mae Brown

Black and white thinking is a method of building fences around acceptable and unacceptable behavior, making all issues cut and dried. There is no shade of grey, no context, and no exceptions. For example, in 1928 baseball great Ty Cobb went into the stands and beat a fan named Claude Lueker unconscious because the guy had hurled insults about Cobb's mother. Cobb firmly believed that his honor and, more importantly, his mother's honor had been insulted. In Cobb's black and white worldview, he had no choice but to lay a beat down on the other guy (who happened to be disabled, confined to a wheelchair, and missing several fingers from an industrial accident). Polarized thinking has no room for context, yet realistically speaking few issues have no room for context.

We recommend:

Take a hard look at your moral code. In much of life shades of grey are appropriate. Take murder for example. Killing someone is clearly frowned upon by modern society, but as horrendous as homicide is there is still an exception made in cases of legitimate self-defense. Are you drawing lines in the right places?

Task of the Week:

Look for a salacious news article, something that is big, controversial, and well covered such as a national election or prominent murder trial and dig deeper, finding at least four divergent different sources for analysis. If, for example, you're in the United States, search for perspectives from CNN, Fox, *The New York Times,* and *The Washington Post.* Then, find additional coverage. Examine the biases of those reporting and try to articulate them. Compare and contrast these perspectives with your own view. It's a lot of work but should prove illuminating.

3. Overgeneralization

> *"On the whole human beings want to be good,*
> *but not too good, and not quite all the time."*

George Orwell

Overgeneralization has been an issue for quite some time, but with today's social and electronic media it seems to be a growing problem. Small aspects of a person's actions or personality are extrapolated out to be an all-encompassing statement of their being. Even "positive" overgeneralizations can be problematic. Overgeneralizing about yourself, particularly when looking at your faults, can have an insidious impact upon your self-esteem. Overgeneralizing about others can lead to snap-judgments, relationship problems, prejudice, or even discrimination.

We recommend:

Similar to filtering, overgeneralization can get you into trouble. Judge yourself and others based on their individual actions and accomplishments, weighing the good and the bad in an attempt to reach a holistic appraisal. There is a difference between who you are and what you do. Even good people make mistakes. Focus on the behaviors. Easier said than done, right? Sometimes the best way to break through emotion is to write things down. The simple act of writing helps you focus on evidence and organize your thoughts.

Task of the week:

Overgeneralization is a dangerous game for a true leader. This week you must look to a group that you do not identify with and learn something about them. You do not need to make this a formal research project; you can do it via the web, a documentary, or whatever you like… just find a reputable source. By the end of the week, you should be able list three attributes that you find admirable about this group. Do the same thing for a group you already find admirable and identify three attributes that you find offensive about them.

4. Mindreading

"It is the mark of an educated mind to be able to entertain a thought without accepting it."

Aristotle

You know what a strawberry tastes like, but do you know what a strawberry tastes like to your friend? You probably think that you know, but you don't. No one can. Projecting what others are thinking, their feelings toward you, or assuming that they think the same way about an issue that you do is, well, mindreading.

We recommend:

This is one of those cases where an ounce of prevention really is worth a pound of cure. If you suspect that something is not correct, it probably isn't going well. Figure out the problem. Don't mind-read; ask the tough questions. If the issue is allowed to grow it only becomes more difficult, more unwieldy to deal with. As a leader it is your job to know the truth.

Task of the week:

This week you are alien to the planet. You are to assume little. Investigation and precision are the tone of the week, to exercise your inquiry muscle and your clarity bones. We've all heard the joke, "Assume makes an Ass out of U and Me." Crude, but true. Probing for understanding, asking for more, and actively listening to others can set up a far more meaningful conversation. That's your job this week.

5. Catastrophizing

> *"All cartoon characters and fables must*
> *be exaggeration, caricatures. It is the*
> *very nature of fantasy and fable."*
>
> **Walt Disney**

Catastrophizing is a youthful emotion, a practice of declaring that, "The whole world hates me!" What parent or schoolteacher has not seen catastrophizing in all its adolescent glory? However, the phenomenon is not limited to youth. Catastrophizing regularly manifests from the mouths of virtually every newscaster, politician, and pundit. Without some manufactured catastrophe looming politicians, pundits, and news people would have trouble keeping their jobs. Certainly, their importance would be reduced. That's why proverbial dirty laundry is front page news. The challenge is that you cannot mitigate a problem that feels so enormous it's unsolvable. You need to get your head in the right place to see it for what it truly is first.

We recommend:

Whether it stems from your own imagination run wild or you are the target of the hyperboles pundit, catastrophizing can be really tough to handle when you find yourself caught up in it. This is when it is imperative to step back, take a deep breath, and try to put things into perspective. Oftentimes talking things over with a trusted confidant, spiritual advisor, or family member can help.

Task of the week:

Catastrophizing is an emotionally immature behavior that leaders refuse to engage in. Your drill this week is whenever you run into catastrophizing, find a solution. Most folks are not self-starters. They want to be told what to do, especially in moments of crisis. This is where leaders excel. Leaders are able to point to a path because they refuse to be caught up in catastrophizing. For the next seven days focus on solutions not problems.

6. Personalization

> *"Don't take anything personally. Nothing others do is because of you. What others say and do is a projection of their own reality, their own dream. When you are immune to the opinions and actions of others, you won't be the victim of needless suffering."*

Miguel Angel Ruiz

Personalization is based around egocentricity; the entire world is shot through the prism of self. It is dysfunctional in many ways, not the least of which is that the self is usually found wanting. If the world revolves around a star player, for instance, it had better continue to do so or there will be trouble. Keeping things from becoming personal is not easy. If the Monday-morning quarterbacks on the sports shows criticize the coaches' decisions, it is their job. By the way, you do know that "Monday-morning quarterback" is a pejorative term, right? Don't take it personally. If they did not have something to complain about, they wouldn't find anyone to watch their analysis. You may be your own worst critic, but you can also be your own fairest judge.

We recommend:

Listening. Yup, listening… and acknowledging the other person's concerns in a professional manner. Those open to feedback virtually always benefit from it even though people giving their opinion don't often consider how hard it is for you to receive negative feedback objectively. When faced with "constructive criticism," strive to look for the constructive and ignore the criticism.

Task of the week:

Your drill this week is to not take things personally. For example, if your flight has been delayed or you've missed your connection, chances are good that you won't get very far with the agent at the ticket counter by saying, "You know this is very inconvenient for me." Try a different tact, saying something along the lines of, "Thank you for your help. I know this is difficult work and that you handle irate customers all day. I want you to know that I appreciate anything you can do to help me get to my destination on time." Replace the frustration of the moment with the circumspect understanding of a leader that this is not about you. This week when you get cut off in traffic, your computer fails, or the mail carrier loses your package, bear in mind that it's not about you.

7. External Control

> *"My helplessness makes my uselessness*
> *seem unimportant."*
>
> **Wally (from the comic strip**
> *Dilbert* **by Scott Adams)**

Feeling externally controlled keeps you stuck. You do not believe you can really affect the basic shape of your life, let alone make any difference in the world. Believing that you have no control over your destiny creates a sense of helplessness and depression. It is easy to get down when outside forces appear to influence every aspect of your life. The aforementioned Filtering and Overgeneralization are culprits in this perceived ceding of control to others.

We recommend:

At the micro level you will always have choices. Outside influences set a context and boundaries, but they cannot control everything. Break big problems down into smaller chunks that you have some hope of resolving.

Task of the week:

Leaders have the characteristic of not letting external events set their tone. They don't complain about things beyond their control. That does not mean they do not acknowledge what is transpiring around them, just that they recognize the context. At the end of the week your attitude and your energy expenditure should have changed with no effort other than this observation.

8. Internal Control

> *"Laws control the lesser man... Right*
> *conduct controls the greater one."*
>
> **Mark Twain**

If you feel externally controlled, you see yourself as helpless, a victim of fate, but that's not the only distortion that can affect your sense of power and control. The second distortion is internal control. The fallacy of internal control has you responsible for the pain and happiness of everyone around you. It leaves you exhausted as you attempt to fill everyone else's needs and feel guilty when you cannot do so.

We recommend:

Know your limits. Good leaders are empathetic to those around them, particularly those in their care, but they can only do so much. You are responsible for fostering an environment where individuals can learn and grow, where talents are effectively utilized to further a superiorordinate goal (such as winning a championship, growing the business, or meeting company profit margins), and where everyone has the resources they need to be successful. You can assure communication, break down barriers, handle politics, acquire funding, train, and mentor, all things that help set folks up for success, but after that it's up to them. Learn to let go.

Task of the week:

Here is your mantra, "Control the body to control the mind; control the mind to control the body." Here's how it works: You can sit anywhere, your office, your living room, even the back of a taxicab, and practice internal control. Sit completely still. Breathe in softly through your nose and exhale out through your mouth. Close your eyes if you want, but it's not necessary. Focus on your breathing and let it calm your mind. Thinking about nothing works great, but can also be a struggle for many. The more you calm your mind, the more your body will relax. This practice should be done whenever you remember to do it. Don't worry about a proscribed amount of time, use whatever you have available this week. Your goal is to build up a Pavlovian response where stillness equals calm.

9. Fairness

"Life isn't fair, get used to it."

**Unknown professor to college
students in business class**

You feel resentful because you think you know what's fair, but other people do not act that way (or agree with you). Fairness is so conveniently defined, so temptingly self-serving, that each person gets locked into his or her own point of view. It is easy to make assumptions about how things would change if people were truly fair or really valued you and your opinion. But if other people hardly ever see it that way you end up causing yourself a lot of pain and ever-growing resentment. If you find yourself getting worked up on certain topics, pay attention to your behavior. Are you turning into a sanctimonious jerk, mocking those who don't agree with you? Lord knows we've certainly done it from time to time. The challenge is that such behavior is not only unconstructive, it is downright detrimental. And, it affects everyone around you.

We recommend:

Have a baseball pitcher's mentality. In order to succeed at any level, pitchers need to have a short memory. If the pitcher is dwelling on the homerun he just gave up as the next batter is coming to the plate, well that pitcher has already lost the game. He is not living in the present moment. The world is not fair, never has been, and almost certainly never will be. Have a short memory. Don't dwell on the past, learn, take the lesson, and move forward. Notice that we did not say move on, because "move on" is a dismissive. Don't be dismissive. Learn and move forward.

Task of the week:

For the next week, every time you find yourself feeling emotional about a subject say out loud, "I'm having an emotional reaction to this." Stop, take a deep breath, and think about why. We're not trying to turn you into a Vulcan, the emotionless race of aliens from the Star Trek television and movie series, but we do want to assure that you are in touch with your hot buttons. This dovetails with flawed thinking around External Control.

10. Blaming

> *"We often spend our time and energy blaming*
> *other people for the problems we see around us."*

Pearl Cleage

Blame is a reverse action, to blame is to look to the past. Leaders learn from the past but focus on the future. It is going to sound very simple, but while you can acknowledge responsibility, you cannot accept or lay blame. Blame is a very low emotion. In blame systems, you deny your right and responsibility to assert your needs, say no, or go elsewhere for what you want. Blaming others makes someone else accountable for choices and decisions that are your responsibility.

We recommend:

Look for solutions instead of blame. It really doesn't matter why something went wrong except to the extent that you are able to identify a root cause in order to prevent it from happening again.

Task of the week:

Look at yourself before you blame others this week. The root cause of an event could fall at the feet of another person, but your job is to look at what happened before pointing fingers or heaping blame upon yourself. The question you are to ask is, "What part of this am I responsible for? Is there a way I could have prevented this?" These are open-ended questions for an open mind.

11. Must

"Force always attracts men of low morality."
Albert Einstein

The word "must" implies truth. If X is true, then Y must be false... Most things come with shades of grey, but not the word must. It is an imperative. Guard the word "must" with caution, using it only when appropriate, even in your own mind. It is easy to get wrapped up in what you must do if you set unreasonable expectations for yourself or others. As a leader you have authority. Even if you are not in charge organizationally, whenever others look to you for guidance your word carries weight and simultaneously responsibility. If not well thought out, hard rules about how others must act can cause a horrible distortion of power.

We recommend:

The word "must" should only be used when dealing with absolutes. When it comes to the grey areas of personal choices use phrases such as "I have found" or "It has been my experience" that provide leeway.

Task of the week:

How many musts do you create for yourself? And how many of those musts are casual? Think of it this way, how many times in your day-to-day conversation do you use the words "must", "need," or "have to" when it is truly not an imperative? It's easy to fall into that speech pattern habitually, so pay close attention to when you use the term must this week.

12. Emotional Reasoning

"I have a woman's body and a child's emotions."
Elizabeth Taylor

Based on the theories of Carl Jung, Isabel Meyers and Katherine Briggs developed a model that breaks peoples' personalities down in to sixteen types. The Meyers-Briggs Type Indicator® (MBTI) they invented is one of the most widely used psychological instruments in the world. It uses scales to chart our natural predilections. One axis of the MBTI scale looks at "thinking" versus "feeling." This continuum examines how people make decisions. People who naturally gravitate towards thinking place a greater emphasis on objective data, whereas those with a tendency toward feeling are more likely to consider people and emotions when arriving at conclusions.

Leaning toward either thinking or feeling is a natural tendency based on your brain chemistry, hence neither right nor wrong, but being on one side of the equation or the other can cause challenges. Consistent, logical, and impersonal criteria are often best when weighing important decisions, even if only in your mind. For example, when it comes to strategic planning, be it in business, sports, or anything else, emotional reasoning simply won't cut it. Emotions play an important role in selling ideas and gaining commitment, but if the underling plan simply makes everyone feel good more often than not it is bound to fail.

We recommend:

The phrase "I feel" is a tipoff that your reasoning may not be valid. Examine the logic behind your thinking before making important decisions or acting on your thoughts. Gut feelings are important, they're valuable survival signals for example, but they are not a basis for all types of decision-making.

Task of the week:

This week listen to peoples' introductory statements to a moment or situation. If the sentence begins with the word "I" it is likely a position of emotion from which they are coming. Here is an example, "I found your words offensive." This is a statement about feelings. Alternately, "Those were poorly chosen words" describes the statement far less emotionally.

13. Resisting Change

> *"Little men with little minds and little imaginations*
> *go through life in little ruts, smugly resisting all*
> *changes which would jar their little worlds."*

> **Zig Ziglar**

While children can be pretty open-minded, adults tend to do whatever they do because it works for them. Their experience tells them that their decision is correct, even when it is not the best choice or even a constructive one. We might feel that our knowledge is inadequate, our skills are not applicable to the new situation, or that we do not have the experience necessary to succeed. Or, we might stubbornly cling to our comfort zones. People tend to be more willing to change given enough pain or pressure that the alternative of not changing is worse, but it is not natural for most to embrace transformation. In fact, forcing people to change when they have not bought in both emotionally and logically almost always breeds resentment.

We recommend:

If you are hoping to create change either for yourself or for your team, you will need to deal with this natural reluctance. This is often an extension of Emotional Reasoning. This means that you not only need to chart the course, explaining why the future state is desirable, but you must also demonstrate success quickly. Without proof that change can and will be successful, preferably with numerous small wins along the way, it is easy to revert back to the original state.

Task of the week:

Step outside your comfort zone this week. The more often you challenge yourself to take risks the easier it will become to do so in the future. Given the speed of change in today's world, resistance to change is not only futile it's often self-destructive. You will miss out on vital opportunities. It is easiest if you choose a worthwhile task that needs to be done so that your risk is meaningful. For example, if you have a fear of heights, for example, go clean a gutter instead of paying someone else to do it. Or stand at the edge of an overlook with a sturdy guardrail and take photographs of the view.

14. Being Right

*"I'm always right. I thought I was wrong once
but it turns out that I was mistaken."*

Any drunk, on any bar stool, in every town

Humans are imperfect, we all make mistakes, yet some folks (probably most folks) are reluctant to admit it when they are the one who has made an error. Always having to be right is destructive in personal relationships. Ask anybody who is in a successful long-term relationship and he or she will tell you about the give-and-take that is necessary. The same applies for your role as a mentor, teacher, or coach. Just because you are in a position of power does not mean that you are always right.

We recommend:

When you are wrong, or have made an error, quickly acknowledge and fix it. Words like, "I was wrong," "My mistake," or the hip, "My bad" are all ways to own up to the error. Willingness to admit mistakes is a sign of strength, not weakness. It may seem tough to admit a mistake, but the truly hard part is working to ensure it does not happen again. Apologizing is easy.

Task of the week:

This week let others be right. So long as their incorrect

position does not threaten your organization or create some irrevocable form of loss, let it go.

15. Heaven's Reward

> *"Happiness is the reward we get for
> living to the highest right we know."*
>
> **Richard Bach**

We all want to be acknowledged. Fame and fortune have a certain allure, but the world really doesn't care about your work ethic, your hours in the weight room, the time you have invested to become a teacher, the degree(s) and certification(s) you have earned, or sacrifices you made to earn the martial arts rank that you have obtained. To assume that at some time you will be acknowledged and rewarded justly for your efforts is tantamount to building a house so that others can burn it down. That motivation simply makes no sense. Leaders who put in the hard work and do the right things impact their organizations far more than most are ever acknowledged for, yet it is the right thing to do anyway. It boils down to intrinsic motivation, a fundamental trait of high achievers.

We recommend:

Sure, sometimes recognition does come with the job, but you cannot count on it. All you can really control is how and when you recognize others. Acknowledge the good stuff when it comes your way and do the things that satisfy you in a healthy manner. Create a healthy life. Because who is living your life, but you? Do not expect reward, but be thankful for it whenever it occurs. Set a good example and who knows, things may sort themselves out better than you expected.

Task of the week:

Do a good deed anonymously every day this week. Tell a coworker about the good job one of their employees has done, pay for someone else's coffee, donate to a worthy charitable organization, or write a positive online review for a product or service you enjoy.

Dojo Wisdom:

> Distorted thinking is as natural as breathing. The key is becoming aware of it. Knowing how and when your preconceived notions are dysfunctional allows you to minimize if not eliminate their impact.

Action:

This is one of those chapters you will likely need to refer back to repeatedly. Whenever you find yourself impacted by flawed thinking go to the relevant section and look toward our recommendations for mitigating the issue(s). Importantly, cut yourself some slack. You could easily go a lifetime without beating all of these tendencies, yet knowing what to look out for is more than half the battle. Diligently performing our tasks of the week should give you the awareness you need.

Stress exacerbates flawed thinking, so it is also important to be aware of what your body is telling you at any given time. In other words, being mindful of your physical stress response can help you regulate tension before it gets out of control.

Do you find yourself becoming angry or agitated, depressed or withdrawn? These are all warning signs to pay attention to. No matter what the cause, it is vital to find one or more stress-busting techniques to help minimize tension and clear your thinking. For example, if you are a visual person, you may be able to relieve stress by surrounding yourself with uplifting images. If you respond more to sound, wind chimes, water fountains, or music can make a big difference. For kinesthetically inclined, intensive exercise routines such as weightlifting, chopping firewood, or hitting a punching bag will help.

Honing the Blade:

Sometimes histrionics are necessary for people to get something off their chest, progress past the emotion, and move on to more productive things. Other times you need to snap them out of it. In those instances, wait for them to wind down and then ask the question, "Why are you not taking action on this now?" Sometimes the act of having to own their words points out to people how extreme a position they have taken in a non-threatening manner.

9. No Fishing off the Company Pier

Six Ways to Separate the Personal and
Professional, and Stay out of Trouble

*"Harry Stonecipher, Boeing's president and chief
executive, was asked to resign March 6th from the
company's board following a personal relationship
between him and a female executive. The company
said its board determined that his actions were
inconsistent with Boeing's Code of Conduct."*

Associated Press

The forced resignation of Harry Stonecipher, president and chief executive of aerospace giant Boeing is a vivid reminder that interpersonal relationships in the workplace carry significant risk. Not only was he forced out for having an affair with a female executive, but when his wife found out she filed for divorce and he was subsequently driven off the board of Paccar as well. This risk is not limited to large corporate entities or traditional businesses however, it is very real and quite significant in martial arts studios as well.

The relationship between students and teachers is complex, especially in the field of martial arts where instructors may hold a higher-degree of power over their students than in other disciplines. While a math or science teacher can flunk, manipulate, threaten, or otherwise ruin their students' lives, they tend to work for institutions with strict bylaws, governance, and oversight. If a professor does something inappropriate, there is a review board and dispute process to follow. Martial arts instructors, on the other hand, have the power to kill. Furthermore, they often run their schools with limited, if any, oversight. Consequently teacher/student relationships in the *dojo* need to be founded on trust, integrity, and honesty, untainted by even the appearance of impropriety.

Because martial arts instructors have a great deal of power, both real and perceived, over their students, it is important that we separate our personal and professional relationships. While intimate relationships between teachers and students should be strictly taboo in any educational setting let alone in a martial arts studio, dating between equals in the *dojo* may be somewhat less restrictive. Practitioners often develop deep interpersonal bonds based on years of training closely together. So long as personal issues are kept from interfering with the smooth operation of the *dojo*, such relationships should not be discouraged. Nevertheless, tribulations in one's personal life do not belong on the *dojo* floor. It is both unwise and unsafe to bring unfettered emotions into martial training. Unlike Mr. Stonecipher, do not let your heart overrule your common sense.

Dojo Wisdom:

> If a relative or family member trains at your school, invite black belts from elsewhere in your system to administer their advancement tests. That not only tamps down any appearance of favoritism, but also helps you fairly and objectively assess performance.

Action:

It is important to establish guidelines about relationships in the *dojo*. If you have not already done so, here are a few ideas that have proven effective over time:

1. **Be professional.** Keep all interactions positive and martial arts-related. Avoid discussing personal matters in the *dojo,* even amongst friends. There's plenty of time in the day for such things away from your students outside of class.

2. **Never date your students.** While there is certainly an upside if things work out, liaisons are likely to cause distraction, resentment, or litigation, and more often than not end badly. Don't go there.

3. **Be even-handed.** If a friend or relative is one of your student's, segregate the personal and professional relationship to the extent possible. Strive to avoid real or perceived favoritism or bias.

4. **Avoid any appearance of impropriety.** When touching students, especially children or members of the opposite gender, ensure that it is done in plain sight. Always have more than one person in the room with you as you interact with others. Whenever possible create a seating area where parents and visitors can watch class without interfering.

5. **Take proactive safety measures.** Like police body cameras and dash cams, security cameras inside the *dojo* can add an extra layer of protection by documenting your behavior a providing empirical data for your defense in the event of a criminal complaint or lawsuit.

6. **Know your limitations.** Resist the temptation to be a priest, counselor, or psychologist for

your students and fellow instructors. Stick with martial arts, it's not only what you're best at, it's also what they pay you for.

Honing the Blade:

A certain degree of professionalism and detachment is always sensible when interacting with students. We live in a highly litigious society where even an unfounded accusation of harassment or sexual misconduct can ruin one's reputation and livelihood. If you teach martial arts, you must give serious thought to potential repercussions before initiating relationships with any student. If you take martial arts, be prudent in dealings with your instructor.

10. Thinking Beyond the Obvious

Three Principles to Harness the Genius of Foolish Ideas

"Innovation distinguishes between a leader and a follower. Sometimes when you innovate you make mistakes, however. It is best to admit them quickly and get on with improving your other innovations."

Steve Jobs

During World War II moving troops to meet the enemy was paramount. Drones did not exist back then and aircraft could only accomplish certain objectives, so without boots on the ground victory was impossible. Simple problem, hard solution... until Andrew Higgins came along. A boat builder from landlocked Nebraska, his innovation changed the course of the war. The Higgins boat he developed is the troop transport that famously hit the beaches at Normandy. While historians laud this innovation as instrumental to the war effort, at the time it almost did not happen.

Higgins' offers to build the troop transport were rejected multiple times. The Navy could not get their heads around the shallow draft, spoonbill design, nor could they understand how a Nebraska native could be boat builder. Despite being rejected by the US Navy, Higgins knew in his heart that he was right, famously telling reporters, "The Navy doesn't know one damn thing about small boats." He also believed that his country was unnecessarily losing lives without his innovation, so he refused to give up. Through the intervention of then Senator Harry S. Truman, Higgins was able to secure a head-to-head competition between his boat and the one the US Navy was using. Higgins' design crushed their rivals' in every test—speed, maneuverability, capacity, etc.

"Thinking outside the box" has become a trite, Dilbertesque statement that has lost much of its utility, which is why we prefer the more inclusive "Thinking beyond the obvious." This simple change of phrase can make a profound shift in your mindset. It leads to the question, "What is obvious?" And, more importantly, "Does what is obvious really solve the problem?" For example, if Higgins had come to the US military with a way to build the same old boats they were already using more efficiently at a lower cost, it would have been equally worthless. Allied troops could not have stormed the beaches effectively and the world would in all likelihood be a very different place today.

Thinking beyond the obvious is based on looking past the established paradigm. It truly is working smarter, not harder. Volumes have been written on how to go about doing that, but in practical reality it boils down to three things:

1. Understanding your goal.

2. Seeking solutions and information outside the norm.

3. Employing diversity of thought.

1. Understanding your goal

What are you truly trying to accomplish? The old saw goes that we never have time to get it right, but we can always find time to do it again. Solving the wrong problem quickly makes no sense, yet it is oftentimes the norm, particularly where bureaucracies reign. Furthermore, the way the goal is stated tends to drive the solution, so be sure to cut to the heart of the matter before you apply resources toward resolving it. This may take extra time and exploration, but it is well worth the effort.

The better you can articulate the problem, the more effectively you can design a solution to resolve it. There are multiple tools that can help such as the root cause analysis, straw man concept, storyboarding technique, affinity diagram, cause and effect analysis, four-frame approach, interrelationship diagram, and the like. The method you choose is far less important than the outcome.

One of the simplest and most effective ways to cut to the heart of a problem is the "5 Whys" technique. Popularized in the 1970s via the Toyota Production System, this strategy involves looking at any problem and asking: "Why?" or "What caused this?" Oftentimes the answer to the first "why" will prompt another "why" and the answer to the second will prompt another and so on, hence the name. In this fashion you not only assure that you're solving the right thing, but also that you can explain the problem in a manner that is likely to drive a successful solution.

2. Seeking solutions and information outside the norm

There is a Japanese expression, "The nail that sticks up gets pounded down." If there is only one "right" way to do things, few people will take the risk to attempt anything different. Groupthink is a tendency within organizations or societies to promote or establish the view of the predominant group. It can be dysfunctional not only because it tends to squash innovation, but also because it downplays individual creativity and personal responsibility in favor of the collective norm. Some of us are willing to take risks, happy to ask for forgiveness rather than permission, but if organizational norms do not provide leeway for measured risk-taking it will become a very rare thing.

It's not just who you talk to, but also how you ask. Oftentimes we attempt to resolve sticky situations by searching for the root cause of our problems, yet flipping things around to look at what is going right can be a better approach in many instances. This tactic is commonly called "Appreciative Inquiry." It helps build on our strengths, just as conventional problem-solving can help manage or eliminate our weaknesses. Appreciative Inquiry follows a five-step process to (1) Define the challenge, (2) Perform discovery, (3) Dream of what's possible, (4) Design a solution, and (5) Deliver results. Here's how it works:

1. **Define**: before you can analyze a situation, you need to define what you are looking for. Rather than describing a problem, however, look for the positive aspects instead. For example, seek "Ways to improve our offense's productivity" as opposed to determining "Why we are not scoring enough points." Your choice of wording can make a big difference; rather than constraining your line of inquiry, your definition should open the option to explore possibilities.

2. **Discovery**: seek to understand what has happened before and the best of what is working well now. Design your questions broadly, making open-ended inquiries that can get subject matter experts talking about proud moments, successes to build upon. Factors that contributed to the team or organization's past successes can be leveraged to build the future. Seek them out.

3. **Dream**: brainstorm what might be. Think about how you can leverage current positives and reinforce them to build lasting strengths. Oftentimes this will simultaneously clarify things you need to stop doing in order to progress, or areas where you can repurpose resources to invest in the future you wish to create. Nevertheless, start with the possible before delving into the practical so that you do not overly constrain your thinking.

4. **Design**: this is where you begin the process of turning the dream into reality, designing discrete changes to processes, tools, systems, strategies, and/or personnel to make it real. Identify what it takes to enable the dream and chart the course to get there. Depending on the scope and complexity of what you are attempting this may require a resource-loaded project plan, though oftentimes it's much simpler than that.

5. **Deliver**: implement the plan. While turning your design into reality is the primary focus, it is important to consider appreciative inquiry a continuous process. In delivering results be open-minded to re-evaluate and continue the process of positive change.

Seeking solutions outside the norm is vital for continuous improvement, without which we and our organizations cannot remain competitive (or even relevant in many cases) over the long run.

3. Employing diversity of thought

This is an extension to previous point, but gets more to the thought process than the organizational norm. For example, if you are a man speak to a woman, if you are a woman talk to a man. It is no secret that the genders see the world in different ways and leveraging this diversity can be powerful.

Going a bit deeper, consider personality types such as those described by the Myers-Briggs Type Indicator® (MBTI), Insights® Wheel, Herrmann matrix, and the like, and make a concerted effort to hold discussions with folks who think and process information differently than you do. Surrounding yourself with people whose brains process information differently than you do can be a catalyst for identifying and implementing innovative ideas, something that rarely happens without diversity of thought.

Dojo Wisdom:

> The more educated and experienced we get the less creative we oftentimes become as we gravitate again and again toward the "right" answer, even if it's the same answer we have used countless times before. Innovation is not always necessary, but developing a mindset that allows you to think beyond the obvious can help set you and your team apart from your competition.

Action:

If you find yourself saying or thinking, "We have always done it that way," it is best to consider why you have done so. If the circumstances are the same, great, but if they have changed in any way the old solution may be suboptimal at best. This is a common challenge in traditional martial arts where classical teaching methodologies needlessly complicate the learning process or obscure context so that practitioners progress more slowly than they ought to.

Strive to surround yourself with people who have divergent backgrounds and experience as well as those who process information differently than you do. By understanding your goal, seeking solutions and information outside the norm, and employing diversity of thought you can come up with far better outcomes than you thought possible.

Honing the Blade:

> Sometimes people are so locked into a way of thinking that they need to fail in order to learn and grow. As a leader it is your responsibility to limit the damage and, without saying "I told you so," move forward to a better plan while keeping the end goal in mind.

11. Don't Fear Expectations

Five Ways to Kill Fear and Move Forward

"Don't lower your expectations to meet your performance. Raise your level of performance to meet your expectations. Expect the best of yourself, and then do what is necessary to make it a reality."

Ralph Marston

Expectations are often feared because they mean that we may fail. But if we never try we will fail nonetheless. Furthermore, if we allow expectations to be managed or negotiated such that they regress to the mean, then in doing so we are made average. Phrases like "It's too hard," "How is anybody expected to know this," or other familiar forms of lowering expectations are so commonplace that one could almost consider them institutionalized. Those who do set high expectations, set lofty goals, and manage their lives toward accomplishing them are oftentimes ridiculed by those who have no goals or low aspirations.

Stay with us for a minute while we touch on a piece of developmental biology called the morphogenetic field. This field is based on the idea that localized biochemical interactions or signals lead to the development of specific structures such as organs. Space and time of an embryonic field are dynamic, but they are defined by the field in which the cell inhabits. In other words, the morphogenetic field for a kidney only allows the cells to become kidneys. Likewise, the heart is only allowed to become a heart when those cells are within the heart field.

In many ways your role as a leader in the *dojo* is the same as the morphogenetic field. When you set expectations and make them obtainable through coaching and practice sessions, then students are able to grow into the field that you have defined. If you set a small field, they will only grow to the edge of it. In other words, with rare exceptions those in your charge will only grow as big as the vision and the expectations you set for them.

By setting low expectations you get low results. By setting high expectations, they (and you) can reach for so much more. There is a tool that has proven successful for this, the SMART goal-setting process. It has been around for a very long time and is widely adopted in Fortune® 500 companies because it works so well. The acronym SMART stands for (1) Specific, (2) Measurable, (3) Achievable, (4) Relevant, and (5) Time-bound. Here's how it works:

1. **Specific:** the goal is stated in precise terms and describes a deliverable or outcome. A specific goal has a greater impact than a general objective and is not only much more likely to be accomplished, but easier to know when you have done so.

2. **Measurable:** what gets measured gets done. Progress toward the goal can be tracked using standards, specifications, milestones, and the like such that you know when/if you have met it.

3. **Achievable:** the goal provides a motivational stretch so that it is a challenge to accomplish

yet possible to achieve. If a goal is too far out of reach you may become discouraged hence unable to maintain the energy or commitment necessary to achieve it. In such instances carve the end game into manageable chunks and set those smaller goals along the path to success.

4. **Relevant:** tying the goal to something that is important to you will help assure a wholehearted commitment toward achieving it. The goal must also be aligned with the team or organization's purposes such that the individual's aspirations support the larger effort and not move at cross-purposes. This is vital not only for teaming, but also for acquiring necessary support and resources.

5. **Time-bound:** tracking your progress over time assures forward momentum and builds in the opportunity to celebrate wins and/or course-correct along the way. The goal should include milestones that determine whether or not you are making progress against a reasonable schedule.

Dojo Wisdom:

> As the old saying goes, people seldom hit what they do not aim for. Given the right opportunity, most people step up (or down) to expectations. Setting lofty yet achievable goals for yourself and those in your charge affords an opportunity to grow. It is far better to aim at a goal and fail, then to never aim and have a mouth full of worthless, "Could haves," "Would haves," and "Should haves."

Action:

Utilize the SMART process to define specific, measurable, achievable, relevant, and time-bound goals for yourself and others. Track progress and meet regularly to discuss how things are going, adjusting as necessary to stay on course. Where applicable, chart a path such as timing and nature of belt testing by rank to assure continuity of vision and alignment of expectations.

Extrinsic motivation (inspiration from others) is great to have, yet intrinsic (self) motivation is essential for long-term development, particularly as you reach plateaus along the way where you may struggle for a period of time without perceptible progress. Publilius Syrus was a poet and philosopher who lived somewhere around 46 BC. A native of Syria, he was brought to Italy as a slave yet won his freedom and education by impressing his master with his talent and wit. He has a famous quote which is apropos here, "Do not turn back when you are just at the goal." This advice seems sort of obvious, but when it comes to overcoming significant roadblocks in obtaining lofty goals all too many folks give up and turn back. This is where the SMART process, when put in place with forethought and planning, becomes most powerful.

Honing the Blade:

> Start early. If your child envisions college from a very early age, chances are good that he or she will make it there one day. If new employees see themselves on a career path, they are more likely to continuously acquire skills and experience necessary for success than someone who has merely found a job. And, if new practitioners understand a well-defined journey toward black belt and beyond, they are more likely to stay the course until they get there.

12. The Circle of Life in Martial Arts

Reasons Why Students Come and Go

*"The study results prove a majority (54%
conservatively) of the reasons why students quit are
beyond the control of the instructor or school owner."*

Gary Gabelhouse

Our interests in *budo* tend to evolve and change over time. As children we may be drawn to martial arts simply because we enjoy the experience. Building strength, balance and coordination are definite benefits, as is a sense of accomplishment as we overcome challenges, receive promotions, and enhance our self-esteem. Our parents likely appreciate the discipline and conditioning aspects more than we do. As young adults, however, we may be more concerned with winning trophies, the tournament aspects of an art. The ability to defend ourselves in a street fight is often a draw, as are social interactions and physical conditioning. As we reach our late 30s or early 40s, however, many begin looking for something deeper, such as internal training, character development, or even spiritual enlightenment.

While most schools offer a range of activities, they cannot be all things to all people. In fact, according to a nationwide study conducted by Gary Gabelhouse that was published on the website fightingarts.com, roughly half of the thousand students surveyed quit training due to reasons that were largely beyond their instructor's control, things like acquiring new job responsibilities or moving to another locality. Others left because they suffered an injury, couldn't afford to continue training, or simply lost interest, among other reasons. This is valuable insight.

Let's face it, students come and go. It's a fact of life and martial arts. Oftentimes it's due to things that are beyond our control as teachers, while at certain times it truly is our fault. Consequently, it is vital to know the difference. For example, those who see earning their black belt as a destination rather than as a milepost along a journey tend to move on to other things once they've achieved that rank. On the other hand, a person who is pushed into full-contact sparring before they believe they are ready is unlikely to feel safe and will probably not return. As martial arts instructors we cannot accommodate every interest, nor hang on to every student, but we do serve a community and need to provide the best product we are capable of.

Sometimes folks tell us why they are leaving, but more often than not they simply stop showing up for class. When possible, it is good to ask former students why they decided to quit, not because there's chance we can change their mind (though that's certainly possible), but rather because honest feedback can help us become better instructors. Regardless of whether we hear it first hand or impute what most likely occurred, it is vital to think about whether we have contributed to driving a student away due to our actions or inaction.

Dojo Wisdom:

> Getting students to help out around the *dojo*, say teaching portions of a class, is an excellent way of lightening your burden while simultaneously driving deeper learning. But, it must be seen as an earned opportunity, not as a burden, punishment, or barrier to growth. For instance, if senior students are forced to spend too much time and energy working with junior ones they may feel they're not getting what they paid for and leave.

Action:

Look for patterns. There are certain times of year when a lot of new folks want to join, and other times when students tend to drop out. You can often see this tied to New Year's Resolutions, summer vacations, school breaks, and the like... That's all relatively normal churn, but if you suddenly begin losing students at a faster than usual pace the root cause will likely be your teaching style, mental state, or the structure of your classes.

While Charles Darwin didn't actually say this, the quote attributed to him applies here in spades, "It is not the strongest of the species that survives, nor the most intelligent. It is the one that is most adaptable to change." If things aren't going the way you need them to, be open to constructive feedback. Discern what is going wrong and make the necessary changes to keep your school and instruction valuable, viable, and enduring.

Honing the Blade:

Most people act in their own enlightened self-interest. While this belief is fundamental to economic market theory, it is applicable far more broadly than that. The key from a leadership perspective is the word "enlightened." When we help folks understand what's in it for them, they are far more likely to get on board and support our suggestion, project, or program. It goes far beyond marketing, but an "elevator speech" that succinctly articulates your value proposition in language that resonates with your customers' needs is extraordinarily powerful for building and sustaining any business or school.

13. Context is Critical

Four Elements of Creating Culture

*"I've missed more than 9,000 shots in my career.
I've lost almost 300 games. 26 times, I have
been trusted to take the game winning shot
and missed. I've failed over and over and over
again in my life. And that is why I succeed."*

Michael Jordan

Context is extremely important. Of all the sports one can participate in, martial arts are unique. More dynamics are in play than in other endeavors. People get involved in the arts for reasons that range from getting enough exercise to learning self-protection to obtaining spiritual enlightenment. Consequently, those crafting a martial arts program must take into consideration how best to serve their students' needs, teach skills that are by their very definition warlike and dangerous, and simultaneously address the legal, moral, ethical, and historical aspects of the knowledge they choose to impart. It can be a significant challenge.

Unfortunately, all too many practitioners overly-focus on content. For example, teaching students how to punch and kick without considerations for the legal aspects of self-defense is like showing someone how to drive a car without ever explaining the rules of the road. It is incumbent upon martial arts instructors to look to the context of what they do. And, to set the culture in doing it.

Most martial arts instructors work with students and fellow teachers who dress alike, speak similarly, and share a common history, just like members of a conventional social club, fraternity, or sports team. There is order, hierarchy, values, and cultural norms in these groups. And, everyone needs a role, a definition of where and how they fit in. Belonging is so important, in fact, that virtually all humans would rather be a marginally tolerated member, the least of any group, than not belong to one at all. For instance, after a few lessons even white belts share pride of membership in their school.

As a martial arts instructor you set the context and help shape the future of those around you. You have the responsibility to take into account the fact that you are providing not only the martial arts content, but the context, which is far more powerful than the actual martial act. Similarly, business leaders, sports coaches, teachers, and mentors have a powerful role in shaping their organizations. Through words and deeds they impact the mental and physical security of those in their charge. Context is vital for setting culture.

The four aspects of creating and sustaining culture include (1) Commitment, (2) Community, (3) Clarity, and (4) Communication. Here's how they work:

1. **Commitment**: this means being bound emotionally and intellectually to a course of action. It is far more powerful and sustainable than mere compliance. People need to believe in the mission, vision, and direction of the organization and be willing to align their goals to help achieve it. Let's face it, students are customers. They can come and go as they please, so no matter how much expert or hierarchical authority you bring to the dojo,

you cannot force commitment. You can create a vision, help folks see themselves in the bigger picture, tie their success to the organization's success, and thoughtfully discuss any concerns or misgivings that might arise however.

2. **Community**: leaders obviously do not act alone. Anyone with a position or responsibility that affects or is affected by the culture plays a role. Sometimes dissenters can become your biggest advocates. If you can bring them into your vision, show them its value and how they fit, and get them wholeheartedly on-board others will see and follow their example. In other words, reformed naysayers often become the biggest proselytizers... Be sure to identify and engage people emotionally where they live, align them with roles that give them the best chance of success and incentivize them to work together.

3. **Clarity**: people cannot work toward something they do not see or understand. To gain commitment they must envision a path to success. Explain the steps involved, how risks will be managed, what support will be provided, and what benefits will result from getting there. As the old saying goes, people who have a "why" will accomplish almost any "how."

4. **Communication**: this sort of goes without saying, but leaders must be effective communicators in order to have any shot at success. You can have a great vision, but if folks cannot understand what you are trying to convey they cannot buy in. This can be especially challenging for certain personality

types. If you are one of them, consider taking classes on communication techniques, acquiring a mentor, or leveraging groups such as Toastmasters International (www.toastmasters.org) to improve your skills.

It takes more than just training, coaching, or lecturing to create and sustain culture. Feedback is a two-way street. Assure robust discussion and interplay such that affected folks can viscerally understand what you're trying to do and how they fit in. Avoid pure facts and data; strive to incorporate storytelling and anecdotes in order to connect emotionally with your audience because folks remember how they felt about a conversation far longer than they remember what they heard. And, whenever possible you must provide opportunities for stakeholders to experience, support, and help build the culture too. Folks own what they create, even when they only play a small role in the development process.

Dojo Wisdom:

> Leaders cannot afford to have a bad day. Sure, everyone is up or down at times, but when you're the person in charge everything that you say or do is scrutinized by those around you, especially your subordinates. You may have the power to promote students, hire and fire employees, hold the purse strings of your organization's budget, or just be a well-respected thought-leader, but either way your opinion counts. Know that you have a position of authority and hold this in your mind as you work through your day. What example are you setting?

Action:

Think about the messages, intentional and unintentional, that your actions convey. What are you doing to the culture, the physical well-being, and the emotional health of those you interact with? You cannot script every moment of your life, but you can pledge to become more aware of the messages you send. For example, a former CEO of Kane's company once stepped in a mud puddle on the way to a meeting and joked about it only to discover to his chagrin that his subordinates spent $62,000 repaving the parking lot the next day. Be cautious of your influence and authority, making a concerted effort to set the example intentionally rather than by happenstance.

A useful tool is the Stop-Start-Continue exercise. Typically administered by a non-advocate facilitator or human resources professional to assure anonymity of inputs, the team is asked to identify behaviors they would like you to stop doing, actions they would like you to take, and meritorious conduct to continue in order to be a better leader. Perform this exercise with your team, listen to the feedback, and make a concerted effort to act on what you hear. This should not be a onetime deal, follow-up every six months to a year or so to track your progress. It helps keep you humble and open to constructive feedback while setting a great example for your team.

Honing the Blade:

> A smile actually changes your demeanor. To truly make the smile effective, however, you need to squint slightly as real smiles goes all the way into your eyes. Try it; you will feel an instant change in your attitude. Sometimes this is all you need to do in order to avoid having your bad day adversely affect those around you.

14. Tackling Insurmountable Challenges

Eight Steps to Achieving the Impossible

"Happiness comes from facing challenges and going out on a limb and taking risks. If you're not willing to take a risk for something you really care about, you might as well be dead."

Diane Frolov

We have a student at our *dojo* who was born with cerebral palsy. As a result, he has limited control of some of his extremities. Given these constraints the student, let's call him Smith, was frustrated with his lack of performance. Wilder was suspicious that the other kids had diminished Smith's perception of his value as a person. Kids, especially those of Smith's age, can be petty and cruel. That's common enough. While cruelty from one's peers can be a powerful blow to one's self-esteem, succeeding in the face of adversity can build it up beyond measure. That is why Wilder felt the need to step in, but he had to be sure that he understood the extent of the challenges that his student faced before he could do anything concrete about it, so he spoke privately with the young man's parents, asking things like:

- "What did the doctors say?"

- "What was Smith already doing to help himself?"

- "What were the parents doing?"

- "How were all these items working?"

During this conversation he discovered that Smith has less than perfect control of his body and that his challenge was never going to go away. Likewise, make sure you have enough information to define the problem, cut to the core of the issues, and place boundaries around whatever it is you are trying to resolve. You don't need all the information, but you do need enough for prudent planning and decision-making.

Armed with a reasonable understanding of the problem, Wilder began to build the bridge. He pulled Smith aside after class one night and said, "You have Cerebral Palsy. It is not going away; we both know that. You really have two choices; you can just roll over and let it hold you down or you can choose to excel. If you choose to excel you are going to have to work harder than anybody else in the *dojo*. It isn't fair and it won't be easy. What you are doing right now is not good enough to succeed, but if you are in, if you are willing to put forth the effort, I will help you. Are you in? Yes or no?"

The kid responded with, "Yes I'm in." Knowing that achieving noticeable early results would start to build a path of success, Wilder then went on to list specific actions for Smith to take to assure that he would be as productive as possible.

How can a person be confident in tackling a challenge if they have not done something similar before or have struggled in the past? If the task at hand is seen as impossible, nothing we say or do will make a difference to the people we wish to lead. Our ideas will be dismissed out of hand, likely not publicly but in the hearts and minds of our team for certain. To build a path to success, we must be credible, honest, and have a plan that opens the door to our vision. And, of course, we must also gain the agreement from our team to follow that roadmap. That's a challenge for sure, but like most things, there is a process. By taking the right steps in the proper order we can increase our odds of achievement.

The necessary elements for creating lasting change include (1) Urgency, (2) Coalition, (3) Vision, (4) Buy-in, (5) Empowerment, (6) Progress, (7) Follow-through, and (8) Success. Here's how the process works:

1. **Urgency**: begin by communicating a sense of urgency. Help others see the need for change, the value proposition, and why action is needed now. Without urgency your plan will continuously risk getting out-prioritized by more important things. Lack momentum and nothing new materializes because it is so easy to revert to the original state.

2. **Coalition**: create a guiding coalition. Assemble a group of thought-leaders with enough clout to get things done. In businesses this is likely to be a steering committee of folks with organization and budget authority, but oftentimes it can be impassioned individuals who are willing to champion the cause as a team. For individual change this is often a support group, counselor, advisor, or specialist who has expertise necessary to help.

3. **Vision**: create a vision to direct the effort. A cogent and pithy vision backed up by specific goals, objectives, and timelines makes all the difference in setting yourself up for success. The clearer you can define the problem and prospective solution the better.

4. **Buy-in**: achieve broad buy-in for the vision. Make sure that as many stakeholders as possible understand and accept the strategy. While a leader can levy tasks, folks are far more likely to embrace the challenge if they play a role in developing and implementing the solution. It takes time and personal relationships to do so, but is almost always worth the effort.

5. **Empowerment**: empower broad-based actions. Remove obstacles to change, attacking any systems or structures that could undermine the vision you hope to implement. Encourage measured risk-taking and nontraditional solutions that further the cause. When working on individual change it sometimes helps to make a "contract" with your advisor(s) such that you feel compelled to understand and accept their counsel even if you are uncomfortable with what you hear.

6. **Progress**: generate quick wins. Make sure the plan has milestones that can be celebrated and recognize the folks who were involved in achieving them. Have a communication plan too; the more visibility of success, the better the chances that others will want to become involved with or support your effort too. Leaders are generally good at reading the proverbial tea leaves, knowing a winning proposition when they see one, so success breeds success.

7. **Follow-through**: see it through until it's done. Align team member's goals and measurement objectives to their role in driving success of the initiative. Measure and hone your implementation approach, using short term

accomplishments to leverage long term wins. In that fashion you can tackle the harder stuff like structural, policy, and system changes using early momentum.

8. **Success**: celebrate the victory. Communicate how the new state makes the organization and individuals therein more successful. Document lessons learned for future efforts. Where possible provide increased opportunities, responsibility, or recognition to those who were instrumental in making it happen. This helps create and sustain a culture of exploration and innovation.

Dojo Wisdom:

> No matter how well respected you are, if a challenge is seen as insurmountable no one will listen to your plans for resolving it. When faced with dire predicaments honestly acknowledge the obstacles and lay out a credible vision for success following the eight-step process. Own it, hone it, and make it your own. With forethought and resolve you can become that leader who overcomes difficulties no one else knows how to undertake, inspiring others to greater heights as well.

Action:

Don't be afraid to tackle the hard issues, but simultaneously don't feel obliged to shoulder the burden all by yourself. Whenever possible, pull stakeholders into the problem resolution process. Not only are those closest to the work intimately familiar with the factors involved, but they tend to have the most skin in the game when it comes to making things better. When you gather insight from these experts, polish it with your experience, and craft a realistic vision you will assure your best shot at success.

Give it a try. Find a systemic problem, some nagging challenge that you have been complaining about or irritated by, and solve it. Resolving a longtime thorn in your side can be the proverbial two bird/one stone victory; it puts the process to work, removes a hassle, and lets you experience how tackling the seemingly impossible can be done via the eight-step process. In this fashion you gain confidence, experience, and credibility.

Honing the Blade:

> Most new leaders hope to make an immediate difference yet rushing headlong into change rarely has the desired effect. Strive to take the long view and cut yourself some slack. It takes time to understand challenges and opportunities, engage stakeholders, and forge coalitions before you can put viable plans in place let alone carry them through to fruition.

15. The Turning Point

Making the Most of a Watershed Moment

"Luck is what happens when
preparation meets opportunity."

Seneca

There is an overabundance of paradigms by which folks perceive the world, yet two are particularly useful when it comes to understanding success and how to go about achieving it, the Lucky Paradigm and the Effort Paradigm. Luck is oftentimes a lazy person's way of explaining achievements. It is a way to rationalize an internal lack of effort and project it onto other people's circumstances.

Here's how this works… If a lazy person looks at another who has what he or she desires, say a boat, the person who owns the boat is perceived as "lucky." The projection of luck as the sole driving factor discounts all the hard work the other person had to undertake in order to acquire his or her resources. Look at the flow of illogical reasoning that takes place with this worldview:

Lucky Paradigm	Effort Paradigm
• You're lucky to have a boat	• I scrimped and saved for years to afford it
• I never get a break	• I made the most of my opportunities
• You have a good job so you could afford it	• I proved myself and earned the position
• You went to a prestigious university	• Good grades and test scores got me in
• Teachers liked you so you got good grades	• I studied hard and turned in my work on time
• My high school wasn't as good as yours	• I got out of school what I put into it

Arguing with a person who lives in the Lucky Paradigm is pointless. You're not going to change their mind; such things must be driven from within. Nevertheless, understanding this perspective can be useful, particularly when taken in contrast of those who make their own luck. Effort Paradigm people understand that turning points are opportunities they can create, influence, and take advantage of, not random acts of the universe.

A "single point of failure" is a concept that comes from manufacturing processes. It is a lynchpin in the system that, if it breaks, will grind production to a halt. The concept can be generalized to mean anything that stops your plans from moving forward. Lucky Paradigm people tend to give up when they encounter these points of failure. They stop and chalk the loss of momentum up to... well, luck, something outside their control. They are resigned to their fate.

While there may be one or more points of failure in any system, there really is no single point of success. It takes more than one thing to accomplish most objectives. What you need to look for and exploit are turning points. A turning point is a time where a decisive change has happened, usually for the better. While turning points are not always easy to discern, adopting a mindset of looking for opportunities rather than focusing on problems makes a tremendous difference. The next time you feel that you are in a situation that has no options, it is likely that your emotions and preconceived notions are in charge. In this mindset you will be unable to identify let alone leverage a turning point.

To get past this we suggest that you take a moment to think about why you are having the emotion. Are you angry, frustrated? Does the frustration, as an example, well up from the fact that you have explained something several times and the person has failed to complete the task correctly? That frustration is a block; it keeps you from achieving your objective. Your goal is not to indulge in the selfish emotion of frustration, but rather to focus on the goal you are trying to reach.

Any time we try to teach others, this frustration can come in spades, but the best teachers make the assumption that failure to communicate is their problem and not the student's inherent lack of intelligence or initiative. Adopting this mindset forces educators to find creative ways of conveying their materials, which in turn makes us better teachers.

Dojo Wisdom:

> Viewing the world through an Effort Paradigm positions you to create your own luck. Don't stop and admire or become mired in the chaos. Your choice of mental model makes all the difference. Look to challenges as opportunities, strive to identify turning points, and exploit them to achieve success.

Action:

If you are struggling to accomplish something, look to yourself first. Is your mindset getting in the way? Is your head in a place where you can get an objective appraisal? Is reliance on the "same old same old" limiting your perspective? Have you engaged the right people, explored enough options, and made a concerted effort to move forward?

It may be time to put things on hold for a while. Temporarily focusing on another problem, project, or task can give you the clear-headedness necessary to see a different solution for your original challenge. Sometimes this takes a few hours, but oftentimes it can take days. Don't get discouraged. While you are consciously focusing on other things, your subconscious mind is still gnawing away at the original problem you were unable to resolve.

For Effort Paradigm people this is self-evident, yet when caught up in the moment we sometimes need to remind ourselves that it's a process. Giving up is not an option. Don't forget that Colonel Sanders was rejected 1,009 times before he was finally able to sell his recipe that launched Kentucky Fried Chicken. If at first you don't succeed… well, you know the rest.

Honing the Blade:

> The old adage, "Let me sleep on it" has real merit. Taking a fresh look at a tough situation when you are in a relaxed state changes the equation, and sleeping is about as relaxed as you can get. Further it allows the sub-conscience to work on the issue in an unobstructed manner. Rene Descartes related that the idea for his new philosophy, The Scientific Method, came to him in a dream. Pretty powerful stuff to have slept on…

16. Break it Down, Build it Up

The Big Bad Chunk and the Three Little Chunks

*"You can break that big plan into small
steps and take the first step right away."*
Indira Gandhi

As a *sensei* you do a lot of teaching. Sometimes that's relatively easy as you know a multitude of ways to explain their materials, but as you've no doubt experienced oftentimes it's really tough. Part of the challenge depends on the audience. While teaching children can be a lot like filling empty vessels with facts and ideas there is little context to leverage, so you need to start slow, explain the fundamentals, and work your way up toward the more complicated stuff. Adults have more context and experience, yet concepts can no longer simply be poured in. New ideas must be fitted into what is already there which brings up a host of additional complications, especially if what they think they know is wrong.

Complex concepts or techniques are best taught as a series of simple principles or movements that, once mastered, can be reintegrated into a whole. We call that "chunking." Like chapters in a book, it segments complicated materials into digestible components. For youthful learners the "bites" may need to be smaller, yet this process can help you succeed no matter what audience you are addressing. Chunking works just as well for conveying knowledge as it does for physical skills, but we'll use a simple karate technique to demonstrate the concept.

Let's say you want to teach a new student a front kick. Your goal is to have the student understand and execute the basics successfully. And, since success breeds success, you want him or her to learn to apply the application as quickly as possible.

Over Chunk: explain the context

We begin with an "over chunk," that is setting the stage by explaining context. For certain learning styles it is vital to understand the big picture before any progress can be made, whereas for others it is not required but virtually always helpful so long as you don't get overly longwinded about it and lose folks' interest. With physical skills such as the front kick this is often done by explaining as well as demonstrating, as this approach plays to both visual and auditory learners. Afterward students get to practice and receive reinforcement, playing to the kinesthetic as well. This combination tends to sink in better than merely explaining alone since it accommodates all the major learning styles.

> *"The front kick is used to strike at a person in front of you. It is a fast kick, a strong kick and one of the 'go to' fundamentals of karate. We will do this kick a lot in our training because it is very useful in tournaments and on the street."*

This talk orients the student by conveying the key elements. And it underscores the importance of what they are about to learn.

1. Chunk One: beginning correctly.

Beginning correctly takes forethought. As the instructor you responsible for the quality of the education. Further, beginning correctly sets your student up for success. Without this you are in for a lot of angst and frustration. A challenge is that if you are really good at something, especially where knowledge or skills came naturally, you may have trouble knowing why. This is the reason that so many sports superstars are lousy teachers; they cannot articulate what made them so good in ways that others can grasp and emulate. Spend time thinking about the fundamental underpinnings necessary to make whatever you are trying to teach work so that you can logically and adroitly explain it to someone who may have a harder time latching onto the concept than you did.

> *"Are you right-handed? It is likely that if you are right-handed, you are also right footed, so let's begin by standing like this with your dominant leg back. We'll kick with that foot."*

It is easier for most people to kick when they wind-up like a baseball pitcher, as they are able to use momentum in lieu of fine muscle control which takes trained effort. By performing the technique with their dominant leg students have an easier time maintaining their balance on their opposite foot than if they were to switch feet and attempt it the other way around. Another alternative to keep from falling over is to have the trainee hold onto a chair or rail. The specific example doesn't really matter all that much; setting the student up for success, on the other hand, is everything.

2. Chunk Two: sequential order.

Starting at the beginning of the processes is pretty obvious, but be thoughtful about the order so that basic actions can be drilled, mastered, and stacked together to become more complex and powerful. Like climbing a mountain there is often more than one way to reach the summit, so in order to achieve your end goal think about the method that is most efficient from the learner's perspective then tailor your instruction to meet your audience's level of experience and ability to understand.

"All kicks begin with a knee lift. The process is to lift the knee up, strike outward forcefully, and then pull your leg back as quickly as possible. We'll just do the first movement for now. Lift your foot off of the floor and bring your knee up to waist height like this. If you bend your support leg slightly it will help you balance. Now you try it. Good. We don't spend a lot of time lifting our knees up to our waist on a daily basis, so it's an unnatural movement but you looked pretty good. Now, a little higher. The higher you lift your knee, the higher you can kick. Let me turn sideways and show you again..."

Sequential order is based on two initial actions that we will begin to stack upon. For physical skills be sure to explain, demonstrate, and let the student practice. If the foundation is solid and the order of actions is logical, the student can quickly add more and more layers onto the beginning point.

3. Chunk Three: stacking.

Stacking comes after the initial move is repeated and done in a manner that is satisfactory. Now we add one more movement at a time. In our kicking example, the next step is thrusting the lower leg outward. To avoid falling down, the student must be able to balance on one leg, lift their knee to waist height, and then extend their foot outward toward a target. As you can see, each of these items utilizes the student's muscles differently for control and balance, yet if taught in the right sequence the movements are easily mastered.

"Excellent! That's pretty good for a first time out. Now when your knee reaches waist height that is the trigger to snap your lower leg outward. Pull your toes back so that you are aiming with the ball of your foot. It hurts to hit something solid with your bare toes. Knee up, strike outward. Let's give it a try..."

Stacking can have as many additions as needed. We like to think of these as data points. Just like making a graph, without the specific data points whatever is being taught will fail. Imagine trying to do a front kick by lifting your knee without thrusting the lower leg forward. It not a front kick any more, it is a knee strike. Lifting your knee and kicking outward without continuing through the progression by pulling your leg back and setting your foot down is ineffectual (and silly looking). As you can see, each data point is essential. When done in the correct sequential order the data begins to flow naturally which is why stacking is so successful at bringing incremental growth to the task.

Chunking virtually any type of new knowledge into fundamental components allows you to communicate complex ideas simply and efficiently. No matter what the endeavor, by breaking component tasks into digestible pieces and explaining each in a logical sequential order you can achieve success far quicker than you may have thought possible.

Dojo Wisdom:

> Try not to correct more than three things during any single training session. Even for highly skilled practitioners, too much information can be overwhelming. It is important to recognize what may have already have been communicated by another instructor as well. If the person has already been getting correction, make an effort to not add new materials until they are capable of processing them. Try to support what may have already been taught by others unless it is fundamentally flawed too; there is more than one "right" way to accomplish many tasks.

Action:

Here is how to chunk using a piece of paper and pencil: Turn the paper landscape on your desk. Now draw an arch from left to right, like a rainbow. Write on this arch the goal that you wish to accomplish. In our example it was, "Teach students how to perform a front kick." Next create three boxes underneath the arch. These are your three chunks. If in filling in the boxes you discover that you've jumped to too high a level, segment each chunk into three underlying components. Once you have the appropriate level of detail, take your completed work to the instructional moment. Follow it and see just how smooth your instruction becomes. It is a great presentation technique too.

Honing the Blade:

> Rather than asking about what has already been taught, have new students explain prerequisites that you think they should know to someone else. Having to verbalize what a person has learned is a great way to drive the instruction deeper. One of the reasons that most advanced martial arts students are obliged to teach as a part of fulfilling the requirements necessary to earn their black belt (or equivalent rank) is that the process of explaining things to others increases retention and understanding.

17. Threefold Mission Statement

Three Steps to Calibrating Your Internal Compass

"An artist is not paid for his labor but for his vision."
James Whistler

Nicola Tesla was a man of vision. He created the induction motor, remote controlled vehicle, radio, and a whole lot more. Even though he died in 1943, Tesla is responsible for the core of much of our modern technology today. Given those amazing achievements you may be surprised to know that Tesla worked as a simple laborer when he landed in the United States after leaving Serbia. Nevertheless, he was not destined to dig ditches any more than Einstein was destined to be a mere patent clerk. There's nothing wrong with using your hands and the sweat of your brow to make a living, but becoming an ordinary laborer is not what most folks yearn to be.

Tesla and Einstein were extraordinary; they both aspired to greater things. But, those two men lived in a different time, not as cluttered and not nearly as noisy as the world we have today. If we want to be like them, we need a tool, a method of building our focus. That's where a vision statement comes in. One of the simplest yet most profound ways to do this is with a vision board, a pictorial representation of your aspirations.

Creating a Vision Board:

One effective technique you can use is the cut-and-paste method, seeking out pictures that create a collage representing where you want to be at some critical juncture in your life. It is better to do that with scissors and glue than to use your computer. Done this way a vision board may sound like a child's kindergarten project, but it is actually a way to reach a deeper place. You see, the human mind doesn't actually think in words, it uses pictures and symbols. If we talk to you about a tree, for instance, you don't think of the letters "T-R-E-E." You think of an image, a representation of a tree.

So, set this book down and build your vision board. Seriously, do it now. When you get done, scrutinize the symbols you've come up with. Is your vision board a physical manifestation of your desired future or merely an aspiration in your head? Think about what each item represents. Does this imagery lead you toward a future of who and what you truly want to be?

Warning: do not read ahead before making your vision board because it will diminish the value of the exercise. Once you're done with the drill, you get to read the next section to interpret your results. To help protect you fast readers, the instructions are written in a simple code to slow you down. Every other word is reversed:

> *Read ruoy vision draob from tfel to thgir now.*
> *Eht items no the tfel side fo the draob tend*
> *ot represent eht items that are ni the tsap of*
> *ruoy life. Eht middle si the tneserp and eht far*
> *thgir is tahw you era holding rof the erutuf.*

This is your subconscious unmasked. Now you have a better idea of what you think and how it matches up to what your mind says about itself in the dark places of your skull.

Creating a Personal Mission Statement:

A vision board is a useful place to start, but for most people it is not enough. If you find yourself drifting, out of sorts, or disgruntled it is oftentimes a result of straying from the essence of who you or what you want to be at your core. Putting your values in writing and referring back to them from time to time helps you stay centered. A great way to do that is with a personal mission statement. This declaration should answer three vital questions:

1. What is my life about (purpose)?

2. What do I stand for (values)?

3. What actions will I take (to manifest my purpose and values)?

1. What is my life about (purpose)?

So, what is your life's purpose? Write it down. Don't worry about polish, just get thoughts on paper. You'll get a chance to wordsmith as much as you need to after you have completed the next two steps…

My life's purpose is: _____

_____

_____

2. What do I stand for (values)?

Values describe your core as a human being, a pretty profound subject. For many it is tough to articulate, but since a values statement cuts to who you are it should not be. The statement should not be long either; oftentimes a word or two will suffice, but the challenge is that it is much tougher for most folks to come up with that one perfect word or sentence than it is for them to write several hundred that are somewhere in the ballpark. Don't sweat it, there's a process:

- Grab a pen and a sheet of paper and start listing what you find important in life. You could type, but many find that the physical act of writing longhand helps them coalesce their thoughts in a more artistic way, with a little more feeling.

- Do not limit the subjects. It can be faith, family, friends, work, a vocation, gardening, sports, education, or virtually anything else… there is no limit.

- Importantly, don't think too hard. Just do it. That's one of the reasons for choosing a pen instead of a pencil, you can't erase.

- Use a timer. Give yourself only thirty seconds to complete the assignment, maybe a minute or two if you're a slow writer. For best success, it needs to be quick. You want a stream of consciousness and not a doctoral thesis.

Like your life's purpose, you may be tempted to edit and update what you have just written but that's premature. All you need at the moment is the brainstormed list you created. After the next step you will pull things together and refine as much as necessary.

My values are: _____

_____

_____

3. What actions will I take?

Now that you are able to articulate your purpose and values it's time to do something with it. How do you make it real? What is the vehicle you can latch onto to exploit the flow of your purpose? Map out the things you plan to do or change near term and long term in order to turn your personal mission statement into a reality. Obviously, this could take a while... It's helpful to begin by drawing a line down the middle of a piece of paper. Label one side "near term" and the other side "long term," and then start writing. Once again, a stream of consciousness is all you need for now. Refinement comes next.

Actions I will take:

Near Term	Long Term

Pulling it all together:

Armed with your purpose, values, and actions, it's time to write things down in a more coherent manner. The key is to hurt your head on it, really think things through, put it in writing, and tweak it as much as you like. There is no right or wrong way to craft your personal mission statement. It is, after all, personal. It should have whatever level of detail you feel is most appropriate to act as your guide.

We have included an example below. Note values, purpose, and actions in these statements:

- Deeply enjoy life, living, and the wonders of creation. Harmoniously balance professional, social, and family commitments.

- Act bravely, courteously, and honorably. Treat everyone with dignity, fairness, trust, and respect to ensure that I am worthy of such consideration from others. Be humble to graciously accept constructive feedback, but do not abide personal attacks.

- Learn constantly. Take responsibility for accomplishments and failures alike, for failure is merely an opportunity to learn. Challenge myself to forever try new things, seek new knowledge, gain new understanding, and ultimately achieve true wisdom.

- Cherish relationships. Make daily deposits in the emotional bank accounts of those close to me. Build bridges through keeping trust, honoring commitments, showing concern, and demonstrating friendship.

- Be a good role model. Demonstrate the virtues of courtesy, honesty, integrity, and service, so that my son will know that chivalry and honor have meaning in everyday life. Be someone my son will be proud to call father and my wife will be proud to call husband.

- Try to give something back. Support social, community, and religious institutions, giving of my time and resources as they are needed.

To be of any use, your personal mission statement needs to come from the heart, not just the head. Much like the collage you built earlier, it should paint a vivid vision of how you wish to live your life, what you want to aspire to, only with words rather than pictures this time. Keep your personal mission statement in front of you and make it real. When you use it to chart the course of your life you will find that you become more excited to get up in the morning, more productive throughout the day, and generally happier at all times.

Dojo Wisdom:

> People seldom hit what they do not aim at. Crafting a mission for yourself helps articulate the purpose, values, and actions necessary to stay on track. Take the time to lay out your plan properly, it may take a week, or may even require a couple of months, but our experience says that winging it on a daily basis or crafting a slap-dash plan that only takes moments to create is a waste of time.

Action:

If you have not already developed your threefold personal mission statement do so now.

Honing the Blade:

> The shorter and more concise a plan is, the more likely it is be followed. The more inclusive and verbose a statement the less useful it becomes. Statements over seventeen words begin to diminish in effectiveness, so keep it pithy.

18. Organizational Mission and Vision

Six Steps to Alignment for a Winning Organization

"The quality of an organization can never exceed the quality of the minds that make it up."

Harold R. McAlindon

A personal mission statement can be a tremendously valuable guide, but any business with more than a handful of employees such as a martial arts school needs that same level of lucidity too. Mission and vision statements supported by well-defined objectives help align actions, getting everyone speaking with one "voice." It can be challenging for leaders to reach consensus because everyone has to agree, but we have found that it helps to start with a "clarity exercise" to align thoughts and identify key words. Armed with this "homework," leaders can have a robust discussion about the future and direction of their organization. Here's how it works:

Clarity Exercise:

Creating alignment is essential to building and maintaining a healthy organization, be it a small *dojo,* a giant corporation, or even a professional sports team. Inconsistencies can confuse and dishearten stakeholders. There are six critical questions that need to be answered to assure that everyone is on the same page.

Answer each of the questions below **in three sentences or less**, enough information to spark conversation but not so much folks get locked into a certain way of thinking due to pride of authorship. These questions have been adapted from www.mindtools.com, which is well worth checking out if you are not already familiar with it.

1. **Why does our organization exist?** *The answer to this question will yield a core purpose.*

2. **How do we behave?** *This question examines behaviors and values required for success.*

3. **What do we do?** *This answer provides a simple, direct explanation of the organization.*

4. **How will we succeed?** *This question requires team members to develop the foundation for a strategy.*

5. **What is most important right now?** *The answer to this question is the establishment of a unifying thematic goal and action plan. Once again it supports development of tactics later on, but it also helps the team craft a vision statement.*

6. **Who must do what?** *This question addresses roles and responsibilities. It supports creation of the vision statement.*

Compile responses from the leadership team and use www.tagcloud.com or a similar method of identifying common themes and thoughts to facilitate discussion. Tagcloud works by identifying key words and displaying them in larger or smaller text depending on how many times they came up during the clarity exercise responses. In this fashion you get a report that shows areas of agreement, at least at a cursory level, without needing to delve into the details of what any specific individual has written. This lets leaders collectively coalesce their thoughts, spurring meaningful dialogue with minimal contention.

The output might look something like this:

maintain team **value** achieve applications **business** company

competitive deliver design **employees** enable

content world class **integrated** manage **people**

products **reliable** partner scalable **secure** technology

standards customers outcomes **information** improvements

empowered **service**

As you can see by this example it is easy to identify common themes, in this instance integrated, reliable, secure information that adds value for the business. That sample came from an IT group, but the same concept applies to a *dojo,* corporation, educational institution or any other type of organization.

Armed with the results of this exercise, you are ready to have robust discussions in which you can develop your organization's mission and vision statements. It's not the answers of this clarity exercise that matter as much as the discussions that take place afterward. The more aligned your thought process and expectations, the easier it will be to collectively chart the organization's future. Mission should come first, followed by vision. Later on, specific goals and objectives will be needed to assure implementation, but we'll just focus on creating the mission and vision statements here.

Creating an Organizational Mission Statement:

A mission statement defines the organization's purpose and primary objectives. Even though it may be shared with outsiders, its function is **internal**, to define and communicate key measures of success. To create your mission statement, first identify your organization's "winning idea." Next identify the key measures of your success. Make sure you choose only the most important measures and not too many. It often takes a lot of refinement and wordsmithing to get it "just right" but it is virtually always worth the effort. The end result does not have to be complicated or lengthy. Try to keep it pithy.

An example of an extremely well-written mission statement comes from Starbucks:

> *"Our mission: To inspire and nurture*
> *the human spirit—one person, one cup*
> *and one neighborhood at a time."*

If you've ever visited one of their stores you can feel the essence of Starbucks in those words, right? And read them on all their coffee cups. Once the mission has been agreed upon and documented, move on to develop the vision statement.

Creating an Organizational Vision Statement:

Vision statements define the organization's **purpose** in terms of guiding principles, values and beliefs. For employees, it gives direction about how they are expected to behave and inspires them to give their best. To create a vision statement, begin by identifying what you, your customers, and other stakeholders will value most about how your organization will achieve its mission. Distill these into the values that your organization has or should have.

An example of a well-written vision statement comes from United Parcel Service (UPS):

- **Integrity**: *it is the core of who we are and all we do.*

- **Teamwork**: *determined people working together can accomplish anything.*

- **Service**: *serving the needs of our customers and communities is central to our success.*

- **Quality and efficiency**: *we remain constructively dissatisfied in our pursuit of excellence.*

- **Safety**: *the well-being of our people, business partners, and the public is of utmost importance.*

- **Sustainability**: *long-term prosperity requires our continued commitment to environmental stewardship and social responsibility.*

- **Innovation**: *creativity and change are essential to growth.*

Once you have solid drafts, combine your mission and vision onto one page and polish the words until you have a statement inspiring enough to energize and motivate people inside and outside your organization. If it takes more than a single page it's too long; no one will read or remember it. Many companies post their mission and vision statements in all their conference rooms, break rooms, and offices as well as on their website. Here is an example from Southwest Airlines:

We operate with a Warrior Spirit, a Servant's Heart, and a Fun-LUVing Attitude

The mission of Southwest Airlines is dedication to the highest quality of Customer Service delivered with a sense of warmth, friendliness, individual pride, and Company Spirit.

To Our Employees:
We are committed to provide our Employees a stable work environment with equal opportunity for learning and personal growth. Creativity and innovation are encouraged for improving the effectiveness of Southwest Airlines. Above all, Employees will be provided the same concern, respect, and caring attitude within the organization that they are expected to share externally with every Southwest Customer.

To Our Communities:
Our goal is to be the hometown airline of every community we serve, and because those communities sustain and nurture us with their support and loyalty, it is vital that we, as individuals and in groups, embrace each community with the SOUTHWEST SPIRIT of involvement, service, and caring to make those communities better places to live and work.

To Our Planet:
We strive to be a good environmental steward across our system in all of our hometowns, and one component of our stewardship is efficiency, which, by its very nature, translates to eliminating waste and conserving resources. Using cost-effective and environmentally beneficial operating procedures (including facilities and equipment) allows us to reduce the amount of materials we use and, when combined with our ability to reuse and recycle material, preserves these environmental resources.

To Our Stakeholders:
Southwest's vision for a sustainable future is one where there will be a balance in our business model between Employees and Community, the Environment, and our Financial Viability. In order to protect our world for future generations, while meeting our commitments to our Employees, Customers, and Stakeholders, we will strive to lead our industry in innovative efficiency that conserves natural resources, maintains a creative and innovative workforce, and gives back to the communities in which we live and work.

When visible, measurable, and managed, a company's mission and vision statements become powerful tools for driving organizational success. To really become and remain real, however, these words need to be backed up by specific goals that are used to align and document individual performance in carrying out the organization's objectives. The last thing we want is for all this hard work to turn into shelfware. That not only wastes time and money, but also degrades our enterprise's opportunities for success.

Dojo Wisdom:

> Whether you teach full or part time, your *dojo* is a business. Like any other enterprise it will have customers and competitors, so a clear vision and mission will help everyone involved articulate the purpose, values, and actions necessary for success. Without such information folks will do their best to make good choices, yet the chances of well-intentioned people making uninformed, misaligned decisions will remain high. Sooner or later this will cost you, often in ways you haven't considered.

Action:

If you don't already have them written down, spend some time crafting the vision, mission, values, and goals for your organization. If such documentation already exists, give it a new appraisal now that you're armed with deeper insight on how to develop them successfully.

Honing the Blade:

> One of the best ways of knowing if everyone in your organization is aligned is to ask folks for an "elevator" speech on what they do. They should be able to articulate everything important in under a minute using their own words rather than relaying memorized messages that somebody else has written for them. If you hear things about the individual's role that do not align with the vision, mission, and values of the group something has gone awry and needs to be corrected. It's probably not the employee who's the problem, but rather the clarity of vision or communication plan.

19. Plan – Do – Check – Act

Measure Twice, Cut Once

"The greatest waste is failure to use the abilities of people... to learn about their frustrations and about the contributions that they are eager to make."

W. Edwards Deming

A popular tool for managing change and improving processes is the Deming Wheel. A pioneer of lean manufacturing and continuous improvement (*kaizen* in Japanese) W. Edwards Deming invented the Plan-Do-Check-Act cycle which was later named after him. A ubiquitous tool in business, particularly where reliable, repeatable processes drive competitive advantage, it is not as well known to or adopted by teachers, coaches, and others who can benefit from it as well.

Here is the process:

- **Plan**: identifying and analyzing the problem.

- **Do**: developing and testing a potential solution.

- **Check**: measuring how effective the test solution was and analyzing whether it could be improved in any way.

- **Act**: implementing the improved solution fully.

As you can see, there are four phases of this process, yet it is not static. One should continuously cycle through the steps as solutions are refined, retested, re-refined and retested yet again in search of perfection. When we follow these steps we set ourselves up to get the highest quality, highest value solution possible for any given problem. And, importantly, we don't get so locked into how we've been doing something that we become unwilling or unable to look at better alternatives. Here's how it works:

Step 1: Plan

First, we identify exactly what the problem is. This seems simple at first blush but oftentimes it is challenging to articulate the root cause and not launch off into solving symptoms rather than fixing the underlying problem. The planning process does not need to be arduous. It can be as simple as gathering our thoughts before speaking to a crowd to something as complex as building a long-range business plan for our company. The point is to clearly identify our goal and lay out concrete steps for getting there.

Step 2: Do

This phase involves generating and analyzing potential solutions. In an instructional setting it might be a single lesson plan. The innovation principle of "fail early, fail often" applies here too. In this manner if our proposed solution does not work out, we have not wasted too much time and effort before moving on to the next attempt. And, we don't have so much emotion invested in our original direction that we become unwilling to make a change.

Step 3: Check

In this phase, we measure how effective the initial solution has been, gathering information that could be used to make it even better. Depending on the success of our pilot, how many improvements we have been able to identify, and our overall scope we may elect to repeat the first two steps or we might launch into step four. That's the goal of the check step, a determination of whether or not we have found a solution that we are willing or able to fully implement. This process was originally designed for manufacturing processes, continuously driving better and better solutions until we have perfected the efficiency, effectiveness, and quality of the final product yet it works equally well for long term endeavors such as honing an individual competitor's skills for the ring. Through testing our strategy and tactics in multiple scenarios we can refine the underlying knowledge, skills, and abilities needed to win consistently.

Step 4: Act

The final step is where we fully implement our preferred solution. It generally does not mean that we have completed the P-D-C-A process, just that we have reached a stable plateau from which to launch our next round of improvements. The process truly never ends as perfection is rarely if ever achieved. Further, with the possible exception of certain products or services with very long lifecycles, changes in technology, regulations, business climate, and the like tend to drive the need for changes in the way we do things. This applies not only to businesses, but also to sports teams, academic institutions, martial arts studios, and the like. The world is not a static place.

Dojo Wisdom:

> It is easy to get locked into historic solutions, the way we've always done things, especially when the old ways worked and appear to remain successful. The challenge is that while historic solutions may still apply, they are oftentimes no longer the best approach. This is where the Plan-Do-Check-Act cycle can really add value. It allows us to continuously evolve by identifying suboptimal situations, testing potential solutions, course-correcting, and implementing the best possible remedies in a timely manner.

Action:

When laying out lesson plans, tackling challenging problems, or implementing long term programs identify opportunities to put the Plan-Do-Check-Act cycle into play. There are few perfect answers. Oftentimes you will need to choose from amongst a variety of potential solutions to test using this process. Use this method to help maintain an open mind, evaluate possible solutions to challenges as they arise, and continuously improve your organization.

Honing the Blade:

> The art of leadership in any type of organization is not checking off on SMART goals, the Plan-Do-Check-Act cycle, grid analysis, or any other tool on a continual basis, it is in understanding the principles and having them quietly operating in the background.

20. Cross-Pollination

Leveraging the Strength of Diversity

*"Diversity: the art of thinking
independently together."*
Malcolm Forbes

Ever eat a Golden Delicious apple? The sweet, yellow colored one? The tree that grows this apple is sterile; it cannot pollinate itself, so it has to have pollen from adjacent apple trees in order to bear fruit. That process is called cross-pollination, an agricultural term that means the transfer of pollen from the anther (male cone) of one flower to the stigma (female cone) of another flower on a different plant, typically by insects, wind, and the like. The result in this instance is a large golden apple that is sweet and good to eat.

Like the apple tree, we owe it to ourselves and those we influence to cross-pollinate. Think about it this way. As a teacher, what can a magician teach you? Put aside the magic act and look at the process... A magician needs to enwrap his or her audience in the experience. What are the attributes of this experience? Is it the clothes? The mannerisms? What about the words that are used, the diction? All these factors are used to transport spectators to a new place, a new world through illusion. Similarly, a good speech is remembered by how people felt, not necessarily what was said or heard.

When looking for a wide range of opinions and perspectives, consider not only the obvious experiential, ethnic, and gender differences, but also generational diversity too. Baby Boomers (born 1946 – 1964), Gen X (born 1965 – 1983), and Millennials (born 1984 – 2002) tend to have different life experiences, desires, and interests, yet they often work together within the same organizations.

Growing up shortly after WWII, Boomers faced more austere childhoods than most of their Gen X or Millennial counterparts, often translating into different priorities. For instance, in many cases a Boomer's parents baked them a cake and invited a few friends over on their birthdays, whereas their own children might have gone to Chuck E. Cheese's or had a catered party. Consequently, Boomers have a tendency to be more conservative, career-oriented, and focus on things that create and maintain a strong support network. Millennials, on the other hand, tend to be far more technologically savvy, experience-focused, and willing to accept change. These varying viewpoints can be very powerful when brought together.

Dojo Wisdom:

> The power of diversity stems from leveraging the life experiences of people with a variety of different backgrounds and thought processes who come together to solve a common problem. It's not just education or work experience, socio-economic, geographical, racial, ethnic, religious, and generational differences are all examples; whatever generates a variety of perspectives.

Action:

What can you learn from the life of a painter? A musician? A movie producer? How do they see their art? Go get a DVD box set you may have wanted for some time, or if you already own a set, you like pull it down and play it with the commentaries on. Streaming video with bonus features will accomplish the same thing. What you're looking for is insight. Listen to the actors and directors talk about their craft, their art. It's a safe bet that they will say something that will jump out, giving you an "ah, ha!" moment. Welcome to cross-pollination.

Honing the Blade:

> By sourcing a position or a statement from a famous person you gain some of their clout. Don't hide your source; share it for everybody's benefit.

21. Owning Your Image

Four Elements of How You Are Perceived

*"People are like stained-glass windows. They
sparkle and shine when the sun is out, but
when the darkness sets in their true beauty is
revealed only if there is a light from within."*
Elisabeth Kubler-Ross

Both authors are fans of the Oakland Raiders football team. Often when people hear this, they try to build a logical bridge to connect the dots. Most think we must have grown up in Oakland, because being a member or Raider Nation isn't entirely logical, not when you live in Seattle with its own NFL team anyway. However, there was no hometown NFL team when we were kids. The closest teams were the San Francisco Forty Niners, who were terrible at the time, the Minnesota Vikings, and the Oakland Raiders. We independently chose the Raiders, followed the games, and even had team posters on our bedroom walls.

When we watched the Raiders defeat the Vikings in Super Bowl XI, well, the deal was made in our hearts. We can still name and talk about the greats, Hendricks, Stabler, Biletnikoff, Allen, Alzado, Plunkett, Long, and many, many more... We keep following them because they are "our team." Love is not rational, be it of an organization, a product, or a person.

Think about brand loyalty, the old Mac vs. PC argument, Coke vs. Pepsi. If you have deep abiding love for your company, your team, your martial arts system, your instructor, your compatriots, your high school or college, or virtually anything else, the fact of the matter is that relationship is a love affair and it's not rational. Nevertheless, it is also very real.

This brand loyalty tends to begin with convenience and the time in life of the exposure. The closer an item it is to us the more accessible it is, and the more accessible it is the more likely we are to get early and repeated exposure. It is close, it's easy, it's priced right, whatever… we make a choice and then, unless it blows up spectacularly in our faces straight away, we tend to rationalize that choice. This is an example of the first impression bias. What started as convenient becomes ensconced in our minds. Over time it turns into a full-blown love affair.

When it comes to martial arts the teacher of convenience often becomes "one of the best." And then the system becomes "brilliant and all encompassing." Clearly the student has made an excellent choice. So, if you are a martial arts instructor, small business owner, coach, or team leader, the question becomes how do you make sure that your school or organization is that prospective client's excellent choice? How do you get them started on that path toward a love affair?

Think about what you are offering. For instance, many Raiders fans are drawn toward the team by their image: iconic silver and black, eye patch, and crossed swords. It's cool. It seems shallow, perhaps, but image matters. Let's break this down a bit, covering the four key elements to how we are perceived by others: (1) Appearance, (2) Demeanor, (3) Attire, and (4) Behavior.

1. Appearance:

Appearance is what we look like. It's not fair, but it's a fact that certain people have an inherent genetic advantage over others.

Nevertheless, we can do a lot about our appearance even if we were not blessed with movie-star good looks. Taller people are automatically given more respect than shorter people, yet a short person with good posture is often perceived as taller than a big person with bad posture. Athletic people are taken more seriously than the obese ones, something over which we have absolute control. Clearly, we can and should make conscious choices about things like hairstyle, visible tattoos, piercings, facial hair, and the like. That's what folks tend to spot first, even subtle stuff like whether or not we have chapped lips and how neatly we trim and/or paint our fingernails.

2. Demeanor:

Demeanor is what we try to look like, our expression. Most communication is non-verbal, so expression is our primary means of conveying intent to others. The rate, tone, pitch, and volume of your voice helps people understand your emotion, which in turn gives cues to your intent. But, it is overridden by body language when not congruent. Since most folks are instinctively good at reading expressions, demeanor plays a powerful role in communication. Not only are we far more transparent than we think, we oftentimes convey a different message than intended. For example, restlessness can be read as eagerness or as nervous fear, depending on the degree. Relaxed body language can seem a sign of cool competence, or of ignorance or laziness. Even how we breathe plays a role. Low, slow abdominal breaths exude competence and confidence whereas breathing high and fast in the chest indicates fear or bluster.

3. Attire:

How we dress says a lot about us. It can tell people about our ethnic origin (e.g., *hijab, keffiyeh,* tartan), give hints to our religion (e.g., *yarmulke,* crucifix, Thor's hammer), our socioeconomic status (e.g., Wrangler, Levis, Jordache), our membership in a group (e.g., red or blue scarves, Masonic rings), or our profession (e.g., uniform, surgical scrubs). It can even indicate something about our values such as whether comfort is more important than appearance or whether it is more valuable to blend in or stand out. Regardless of our physical beauty, intelligence, or physique, neatly pressed clothing conveys a different impression than a rumpled appearance. And, a martial arts instructor whose uniform is covered in patches and "bling" gives a very different impression than one whose starched white uniform *gi* is devoid of ostentation.

4. Behavior:

Behavior, appearance, and speech interact. Lots of things come out naturally in our behavior. For example, how we move gives insight to your physicality, our comfort with ourselves, and how we feel about other people. How we stand shows whether we are prepared or unprepared, if we are on top of things or lax. Non-verbal behavior sends a powerful message when communicating with others. Some folks, especially those who are kinesthetic learners, tend to have body language that is naturally dismissive of others even when they are paying rapt attention. Are you multi-tasking or actively listening, making direct eye contact or staring off into space, leaning forward or sitting back with your arms crossed? To be perceived as sincere, it is vital to be aware of how you are coming across and have as congruent of a message as possible.

Dojo Wisdom:

> Leaders who are viewed as cold, calculating, or indifferent have a very hard time getting anything done even when they are earnest and forthright. Since nonverbal communication trumps words, it is imperative to be conscious and considered about the impression you give.

Action:

Image is an admixture of appearance, demeanor, attire, and behavior, all factors that you control to large degree. What you do, the manner in which you dress, how you act and react—purposeful or not these elements all play powerful roles in how others perceive you. Perception being reality in most instances, this means that image can help or hinder your ability to meet personal and professional goals. Choose wisely.

Honing the Blade:

Colors can affect how you are perceived. There are two basic skin tones, warm and cool. A neat trick for identifying which category you fit into is to look at the veins underneath your arm. If they show blue through your skin you have cool tones, whereas if they are more greenish in appearance you have warm tones. Knowing your skin tones can help you select clothing (and cosmetics) that augment your appearance. Be aware of what you wear where, however. For example, the wrong color clothing can incite hostility or violence at a sporting event even if you aren't rooting for the other team.

22. Use New Methods

Avoid Getting Stuck in the Past in the Name of Tradition

"I must study politics and war that my sons may have liberty to study mathematics and philosophy. My sons ought to study mathematics and philosophy, geography, natural history, naval architecture, navigation, commerce, and agriculture, in order to give their children a right to study painting, poetry, music, architecture, statuary, tapestry, and porcelain."

John Adams

The speed of change is ever increasing nowadays, but it hasn't always been that way. In fact, it's a safe bet that your great, great, grandfather and your grandfather lived very similar lives, yet your children's will be very different than your own. For example, the authors grew up before personal computers and the internet, yet our children have owned smartphones thousands of times more powerful than our first PCs their whole lives. To put things into perspective, Neanderthals did not change much for about 250,000 years, that's roughly 8,333 generations, yet in just a single generation Homo Sapiens, that's us, went from the Wright brothers' twelve-second flight at Kitty Hawk in 1903 to Chuck Yeager breaking the sound barrier in 1947.

Passing on information is an essential part of any society and every individual's growth and development. Long chains of information must be strung together in relatable and repeatable forms for success. Initially it's a simple, "If this then that" formula that the Neanderthals surely used. But, that's not enough. At some point the creativity and wisdom of the individual comes into play.

Historians lament the burning of the library of Alexandra, once the world's greatest storehouse of knowledge in 40 BC, yet today we dwarf that ancient library with materials on the World Wide Web. Modern universities want to survive and they do that by offering ever evolving educational experiences and teaching methodologies designed to reach their target audiences. E-learning, interconnected classrooms, gamification, and immersive simulations are commonplace. Don't ignore this example of how education has changed when you walk through your *dojo* door.

Why the history lesson? Teaching martial arts to today's generation using methods from even one generation ago is a formula for a train wreck at your expense. Millennials learn very differently than Boomers and Gen-Xers. Simply put, it's a new time with new students and new expectations. Ancient methods of instruction have value, but must adapt to the world we currently live in. To ignore this new form of information is the equivalent of saying, "That wheel thing is nice, but I just don't see it catching on."

Dojo Wisdom:

> Every Olympian, every professional athlete, and every successful business leader in today's world has a method and a means of stepping outside their chosen arena to find what's necessary to improve, yet in many studios martial arts are still taught in the same "tried-and-true" fashion that was popularized by their founder generations ago. Why are you depending on old methods to reach new minds? If you are using modern methods, can they be updated?

Action:

Take a hard look at your curricula. Are you passing on "secrets" or holding things back? Are you addressing student needs and individual learning styles? Are you showing techniques without providing context or explaining why? In other words, are you making it harder than it has to be for folks to learn your art?

You may be getting tired of football analogies, but hey, we played, our kids played, and we're lifelong fans. So, here's another one, but it's apropos… American football was invented in the late 1800s, roughly the same time period during which many traditional martial arts were codified, yet it has not remained static. The rules of the sport have evolved over time, adding passing to the running game for instance. The ways in which athletes hone their skills in practice have changed significantly as well.

Consider how winning coaches prepare their teams to perform on the field through instrumentation, video evaluation, and structured exercise that is tailored for each position. Be sure that you're similarly taking advantage of modern technologies and training methods to help your students excel.

Honing the Blade:

> People have a tendency to needless complicate
> things in order to appear smarter, wiser, or more
> accomplished, yet the mark of true mastery is the
> ability to explain complex concepts or ideas in simple
> terms that virtually anyone can understand.

23. The Right Words

Verbiage is More Important than You Might Think

"Nobody cares how much you know, until they know how much you care."

Theodore Roosevelt

Men and women see the world differently. They have different brain chemistry, hence have a tendency to process information and respond to words in different ways. What motivates a man is not as likely to motivate a woman and vice versa. This is neither a bad thing nor a good thing, just a difference—different brains, different needs. There are numerous examples of gender brain differences. A study done by Larry Cahill, a professor at the University of California, Irvine, proves this point. His research demonstrated that brains of men and women respond differently to horror films by tracking neural activity in the amygdala.

Located deep in the temporal lobes of the brain (behind the eyes and about where your temples are), the amygdala controls emotional reactions. Professor Cahill was able to demonstrate that when the male subjects were exposed to a horror film, the left side of their amygdala lit-up. That side is responsible for accounting for the basics of the event a person is witnessing, the essence of the moment. When women were exposed to the same scene, however, the opposite side of their amygdala fired. The right side of the amygdala is in charge of the details of the moment.

The result of these differences might be that when a couple sits in a theater watching a scary movie, the boyfriend is thinking about what the characters should be doing to get out of the house, clear the threat, and escape to safety. The girlfriend, on the other hand, is noticing that the distribution of the blood splatter that was on the left side of the actor's face in the previous scene has suddenly switched sides due to an editing error… all while simultaneously trying to figure out how to clear the threat and escape to safety. Different responses by gender to the same stress, the same information, make it evident that although the same general area of the brain is engaged, the location utilized varies so the reactions are different.

Similarly, there is a difference in gender when it comes to teaching. Men and women tend to respond differently. There are many ways to approach this to improve your teaching, but one of the simpler and most direct ways to be successful is to understand the way the genders generally desire things:

- Most men want to know that they are strong and also that they are at the very least competent. Men can live with not being the best at everything, but if you look closely, you will see that men will carve out a niche in which they are proficient. So, if work doesn't reflect this competency, a hobby usually will.

- Most women, on the other hand, prefer to be beautiful and loved. They don't have to be the most beautiful woman in the room, but they do need to be the most beautiful to those that they love and who love them back. In our experience there is no greater love or joy exchanged than that of a young child with and for his or her mother. The mother is the most beautiful person in the world to the child and vice versa. This illustrates the point we are making.

Because the mind hears the action and the noun, Wilder uses a communication trick when talking with students of different genders to assure that they understand his intent. Let's say that he wants to compliment the student for performing a properly executed karate punch, here is an example of how the two different approaches might work:

Men: *"Jason that was a strong punch. Solid form."*

Women: *"Laura that was a beautiful punch. Good form."*

Jason heard the words, "strong" and "solid" whereas Laura heard, "beautiful" and "good." This is an example of speaking to the genders in different words in order to obtain the same result, clear communication. Finding the right words can be tough enough at the best of times, yet in stressful situations it can be a significant challenge. A great resource is the book *Effective Phrases for Performance Appraisals* by James E. Neal, Jr. While written for a specific managerial responsibility, the concepts apply broadly. Additionally, here is a short list of words that you can use to spark the right conversation:

- Strength
- Confidence
- Goals
- Consistency
- Imagination

- Believe
- Challenge
- Fulfillment
- Risk
- Pride
- Discipline
- Drive
- Hard work
- Action
- Joy
- Passion
- Knowledge
- Overcome
- Role model
- Encouragement
- Own it
- Great
- Control
- Action

Choosing the right words is important, but you must also consider your audience when you speak in order to select the right approach. For example, many business executives prefer a "be bright, be brief, be gone" methodology, whereas many lower-level managers and technical people feel a need to know and analyze all the relevant details. These differences are based both on brain chemistry as well as schedule availability.

Regardless of the level of detail expected, knowing where you are leading to will help clarify your arguments and tighten up conversations. It works much like a common practice in behavioral interviewing where applicants are asked to answer questions in the form of a STAR, an acronym that stands for (1) Situation, (2) Task, (3) Action, and (4) Result. Using the STAR technique forces a logical, structured response that can crisply explain what occurred, giving interviewers pertinent information necessary to evaluate and differentiate candidates.

On or off the job, words can spark conflict in all aspects of your life. Being sanctimonious, condescending, dogmatic, or derogatory tends to get other people's dander up rather quickly. Praise publically, criticize privately.

Dojo Wisdom:

> People often don't hear the modifiers in conversations. Similar to predictive typing used by many computer applications and smartphones, the human mind makes assumptions about the sentence that has just been spoken, oftentimes glossing over the modifiers and focusing only on the subjects and actions. To counter this, speak in positive terms. The classic example is the coach who says, "Don't fumble the football," instead of using the more constructive approach, "Hang on to the ball." The former could backfire whereas the latter is far less likely to be misunderstood.

Action:

It's not always legal to record your conversations, but reviewing what you've said through a digital recorder or via streaming media can prove enlightening. If that's not possible, ask a close friend or associate to describe the words or phrases you use most often. You see, habitual turns of phrase often come back to haunt us. For example, saying something along the lines of, "Let me be honest with you," or "Truthfully...," implies that up until that point in the conversation you have been deceitful, even when you were completely forthright. It's important to know if you're unknowingly doing something like that.

Ambiguous words like "kinda," "sorta," and the like may have their place, particularly amongst friends, but they come across as indecisive in more professional settings, hence can undermine our credibility. The phrase "you know" is often annoying. After all, if the audience already knows, why are you saying it? Everyone stumbles from time to time, especially when searching for the exact right words to convey a thought, but excessive use of "um," "uh," and "and" will make us seem insecure. To become excellent communicators, we must strive to drive these dysfunctional quirks out of our vocabulary.

Honing the Blade:

> The word "problem" implies great difficulties, something seemingly insurmountable. The word "challenge," on the other hand, implies something more easily overcome. Replace the word problem with the word challenge and you will be seen as a more optimistic individual. It helps place you in the mindset to identify creative solutions too.

24. Brain Typing

Chess Trumps Checkers When
it comes to Personnel

*"There is no substitute for accurate
knowledge. Know yourself, know your
business, know your men."*

Lee Iacocca

We all know that checkers and chess both use exactly the same game board, yet the rules are significantly different. In checkers, all pieces are treated the same, hence become interchangeable. This drives very different strategies than we find in chess where we are able to make use of the unique strengths and weaknesses of the various pieces to play the game. While high performing organizations use their human resources like chess pieces, all too many groups play checkers with their personnel, forgoing the unique leverage afforded by optimally utilizing the knowledge, skills, and experience of each individual. This does a disservice to both the people and the organization.

For those who follow American football, you know that both John Madden and Pete Carroll demonstrated the power of adjusting their strategy to the strengths and weakness of their players rather than trying to force fit folks in to the coach's schema. And, they have both won Super Bowls using collections of misfits and miscreants who were rejected by other teams. Let's face it, all professional players are superior athletes, but their performance is affected both by their attitudes and brain types. Understanding how this works creates the margins between success and failure at the highest levels.

By understanding brain typing you can help the little league player, the college athlete, or the professional. And, you can use it to help yourself too. The science behind this was popularized by Jon Niednagel, President of the Brain Typing Institute. Volunteering as a youth soccer coach, he noticed that players who behaved similarly also had similar athletic techniques. From there, he began to connect the Myers-Briggs Type Indicator® (MBTI) brain types to athletic performance on the field.

The MBTI was developed by the mother and daughter combination of Isabel Myers and Katherine Briggs in an effort to operationalize the theories of renowned psychiatrist Karl Jung. It was used during World War II for successfully placing civilians in jobs required by the war effort and has been refined several times since. Constantly being tested for validity and reliability, it has been widely adopted by businesses, sports teams, and academic institutions today. The theory goes that each person is born with one of 16 brain types. These types are based on four basic pairs of psychological attributes which operate along continua, meaning that any individual can be anywhere from one extreme to the other along the scale. These predilections include:

- Extroverted (E) vs. Introverted (I)

- Sensing (S) vs. iNtuitive (N)

- Thinking (T) vs. Feeling (F)

- Judging (J) vs. Perceiving (P)

Each brain type combination has inherent strengths and specific weaknesses, qualities that affect all aspects of a person's life and are particularly apparent in physical endeavors like football or martial arts. With over twenty years of research on psychology, neuroscience, and biology, Niednagel codified his theories and became an adviser for professional sports teams throughout the United States. In one of his most famous predictions, he helped the Indianapolis Colts select Peyton Manning (ESTP) in the 1998 draft, stating that he would become a top performing quarterback in the NFL, whereas Ryan Leaf (ESTJ) would be much less successful because of his personality type.

You probably know how incredibly well that selection worked out, but in case you haven't heard Manning recently retired after winning the Super Bowl as quarterback for the Denver Broncos. Former number two overall draft pick Leaf, on the other hand, had a short-lived professional career that earned him the reputation as one of the biggest busts in NFL history. Since leaving football he has had several run-ins with the law, including a 2012 arrest for breaking into two houses and stealing painkillers while on probation for other crimes. In 2013 he was moved from a drug treatment center to the Montana State Prison for threatening a staff member and other behavioral problems according to news reports. Reformed, Leaf now works with the treatment center he credits with his sobriety and new lease on life.

When you discover that athletes' personalities can be assessed through their body motions on the field, you begin to realize that psychological type has its underpinnings not only in the brain, but throughout one's entire body. This is powerful information. Niednagel has been able to identify athletes' personality types in mere minutes simply by watching how they move. He also uses electroencephalography (EEG) scans for verification from time to time, relying on hard science to augment psychological theory. Under the EEG it is possible to see that different personality types use certain regions of their brains differently. For predicting athletic performance Niednagel organizes MBTI personality types by their middle two letters since those are the ones that most affect physical skills. In other words:

- SFs (Sensing-Feeling) tend to be gross-motor skilled.

- STs (Sensing-Thinking) tend to be fine-motor skilled.

- NFs (iNtuitive-Feeling) tend to be speech-skilled.

- NTs (iNtuitive-Thinking) tend to be voice-skilled and adept at logical abstraction.

Professional athletes and coaches alike have gravitated toward this approach because it works. Research shows that roughly 60% of athletic ability stems from personality predilections, whereas the remaining 40% comes from environmental factors such as team cohesion and effective coaching which you can control, and the way the person was raised, their value system, and support from family and friends over which you will have minimal, if any, influence. To delve a little deeper, here are successful strategies for coaching folks with various brain types:

- **Extraversion** (E): successful strategies for working with extraverts generally include interactive assignments using collaborative work groups, freeform discussions or debates to exchange information and stimulate learning. These folks often prefer oral communication over written.

- **Introversion** (I): for introverts it is important to integrate and connect subject matter, using logical chunks of interconnected facts. These individuals generally prefer to think and reflect on work, excelling at written assignments while being challenged by interactive discussions. When debate is required, allow sufficient think time for Introverts to deliberate ahead of time.

- **iNtuition** (N): intuitive people like more generalized concept maps and learn well using a "theory–application–theory" approach. These individuals are comfortable working with hunches and other unexplainable ways of knowing, looking for patterns, meanings, and future possibilities. While they excel at creative assignments, they are often bored by, and resistant to, routines.

- **Sensing** (S): strategies for interacting with sensing individuals include organized, linear, structured discussions conducted in an "application–theory–application" approach. These folks tend to appreciate early understanding of objectives so that they can prepare for what they must know or do in advance. They prefer to work with givens in the real world rather than with abstract theories or possibilities.

- **Thinking** (T): thinking individuals generally focus on facts and data. They strongly believe in, and generally want to comply with, objectives, principles, and policies and may have trouble working "outside of the box." They have a strong preference for organizing and structuring information in logical, clear, and objective ways, and working toward precise, action-oriented assignments.

- **Feeling** (F): feeling individuals tend to be subjective, values-based people, who focus on emotion rather than fact. They have preferences for organizing and structuring information in a personal, value-oriented ways. Successful strategies for working with these individuals include interactive group activities, open discussions, and harmonious social interactions.

- **Perceiving** (P): because individuals who prefer perceiving are flexible and open to experience, they often have many things going on at once but do not always follow through. Successful strategies for these folks include breaking assignments into small steps with interim deadlines to assure completion. These individuals excel in situations that allow for spontaneity and creativity.

- **Judging** (J): people who prefer judging like to analyze, organize, and respond, often testing conventional theory. They are goal oriented and enjoy situations that are organized and scheduled. Leaders who play the "devil's advocate" and encourage reverse questioning or debate are often appreciated. Assignments for such individuals should be well-structured with activities and timeframes prearranged.

When you are not dealing with folks one-on-one or in small groups of like-minded individuals, it is particularly helpful to focus on only two of the scales, Extraversion (E) vs. Introversion (I), and Sensing (S) vs. iNtuition (N). These scales have wide ranges, so while folks gravitate one way or the other, they are not all exactly alike. Nevertheless, these predilections are almost always visible if you know how to look for them. Here's how it works:

- **Extraverted** (E) people draw energy from outside themselves, thriving on interactions with people, activities, and things. They actively participate, ask questions, and get involved. They also have a tendency to monopolize your time and attention by asking a disproportional number of questions or engaging in prolonged discussions.

- **Introverted** (I) people, on the other hand, draw energy from their internal world of ideas, emotions, and impressions. They tend to be reflection oriented, learning best in a "think-do-think" environment. Even when they are thoroughly engaged, they may appear distant, distracted, or a step behind the others. Introverts are often uncomfortable asking for help and must sometimes be actively drawn into conversations.

- **Sensing** (S) individuals naturally gravitate toward the practical and the immediate. Their learning styles are characterized by a preference for direct, concrete experiences, moderate to high degrees of structure, linear or sequential learning, and a need to know why before doing something. They are often less independent in thought and judgment and may require frequent coaching or direction.

- **iNtuitive** (N) individuals are generally "big picture" types who prefer to focus on imaginative possibilities rather than on concrete realities. This personality type likes to move from theory to practice, typically disliking highly structured environments. They readily accommodate ambiguity, demonstrating a large degree of autonomy and valuing knowledge for its own sake.

By understanding brain types of those in their charge, teachers, coaches, and mentors can communicate better with their teams. Further, they can best align personnel with assignments or positions where they are most likely to excel, one of many ways to leverage a team or organization's strengths and shore up their weaknesses.

Dojo Wisdom:

> Your brain type isn't static, it can change over time. What you value in life and how you approach it often transforms. For example, as adults we may enjoy a good merlot wine, whereas as teenagers we liked Dr. Pepper. Be aware that brain plasticity, age, responsibility, and social environment can change your brain in many ways, some of which may show up on a personality test.

Action:

There are lots of online personality tests, and many are valid, yet as stated previously we prefer the Myers-Briggs model as we have found it consistently reliable, insightful, and actionable. You can take the test on a variety of sites, yet some require registration or charge a fee. The link we suggest, 16 Personalities (www.16personalities.com), is a great resource. It can be as in-depth as you wish to go, suggesting career paths, work methods, and relationship styles. Importantly, as of this writing it is personal, private, and free. You can also visit the following web sites for more information on MBTI: www.advisorteam.com, www.keirsey.com, or www. capt.org. Take the MBTI test, and if you can, have the folks in your organization take the test as well. The results will prove illuminating.

Honing the Blade:

Brain types are predilections, not immutable traits. Kane once worked for a vice president who completely misunderstood how to use MBTI information, hence promulgated that all teams be comprised of a specific combination of personality types. It should come as no surprise that the mandate was a spectacular failure, rescinded after three or four months to the embarrassment of the guy who issued the order. It is important to understand this information, but at the same time not to become bound by it.

25. Recognizing Effort

Five Fundamentals of the Morale Imperative

*"The magic formula that successful businesses
have discovered is to treat customers like
guests and employees like people."*

Tom Peters

Are you linking recognition to specific actions or behaviors that support your organization's goals and values? According to exit interviews, one of the primary reasons that people leave their job is lack of recognition for their contributions. Bad management plays a huge role as well. Clearly those two factors go hand-in-glove. And, the same thing applies in martial arts studios.

Some folks are more motivated by a challenging assignment than they ever would be from a cash award or stock option. Acknowledgement can be anything from a kind word to a rank certificate, patch, or belt. It's not the recognition so much as how and when you do it that matters. Like goal setting, recognition should be SMART. Yes, we're using that acronym again, but this time the five elements stand for (1) Sincere, (2) Meaningful, (3) Adaptable, (4) Relevant, and (5) Timely. Here's how it works:

1. **Sincere**: this is sort of self-explanatory, but even sincere recognition can seem disingenuous if you don't do it right. Be specific about the behaviors or results that you value rather than offering generalized praise. Explain what was done, why it matters, and how much it means to you that the person did it.

2. **Meaningful**: any award should enhance the recognition, not be the recognition. Recognize others by showing respect, asking for input, giving feedback, providing opportunities, or just saying "thank you." Consider who and how to deliver the acknowledgement so that it will have the most meaning and impact. In hierarchical organizations, for instance, formal recognition events can provide career-affirming "face time" with key decision makers. Personalization makes it more meaningful too.

3. **Adaptable**: different people like to be recognized in different ways. For some a public event is embarrassing whereas others cherish the attention. Some people would be thrilled to receive football tickets, while others might prefer to attend the movies, an opera, or dinner theater. The better you know your team the better you can reward them in ways they will find meaningful and the better you can deliver appropriate recognition in alignment with individual predilections such as a preference for public or private recognition.

4. **Relevant**: keep the recognition appropriate in size for the achievement. Awarding 10,000 shares of stock for performing a routine job assignment is inappropriate, we all know

that, but sometimes it is hard to directly tie recognition to the organizational impact of a person's actions. Don't overthink it; simply assure that every individual feels valued for their contributions, recognition is relevant with accomplishments, and that you are consistent in how and when you demonstrate appreciation to the team.

5. **Timely**: this may seem like a no-brainer, but if you work in a large organization, it can take forethought and proactive action in order to work through the bureaucracy and receive approval to recognize employees in timely manner. Incorporate recognition planning into your operating rhythm so that you are always on the lookout for meritorious behaviors and have mechanisms in place to suitably recognize them in a timely manner.

Hold everyone to established standards of performance at all times, recognizing laudable behaviors and correcting inappropriate ones in a timely manner. Clearly you do not want to publically embarrass anyone who gets out of line, save in very rare circumstances, but oftentimes escapes can become learning moments, opportunities to improve processes, tools, or policies, or to send a powerful message about appropriate and inappropriate behaviors to the team. Don't let things slide. If you recognize bullying behaviors from a student during tandem drills, for instance, correct that immediately or right after class. The longer it goes on the harder it is to ameliorate. And, the more acceptable it becomes to those who witness it.

Above all, be consistent! If you appear to be playing favorites the recognition effort will backfire. Often spectacularly. Never forget that team members talk to each other. If you are not fair, objective, and consistent in how you apply recognition they will know. Few things undermine team cohesion and morale more than favoritism.

As you think about others, do not forget about recognizing yourself. This isn't about self-aggrandizement, but rather about maintaining your mental and physical health and well-being. Burn-out can be overlooked by self-starters, folks who have an overdeveloped sense of responsibility hence put their organization or team ahead of their own self-interests too often. They might start feeling the indicators of burn-out but ignore them to their detriment. Some of the warning signs include:

- **Cynicism**: you find yourself becoming pessimistic, always looking for the negatives in any situation. A famous radio personality once told Wilder, "Nobody wants to hear if a DJ had a bad day. If they keep bringing it up, nobody will hear about it because that DJ will be out of a job."

- **Low energy**: you are dragging yourself to meet your goals. Often achievers will attribute this to their own failure(s). They will pump themselves up, mentally beat themselves up, and do whatever it takes to handle what they see as their shortcomings. Low energy is not always a function of poor health or bad nutrition; it can come from emotional drainage too.

- **Quick to anger**: if you find that you are uncharacteristically quick to anger pay attention. It's hard to be around folks who lack patience and have a short fuse. If the situation continues it will create distance between you and those around you. Audit yourself and ask, "At what point did I start to become so angry?"

- **Self-medication**: some people reach for assistance beyond a cup of coffee or Red Bull® to get up and get tasks done. If alcohol or drugs have become a crutch, you have a problem with burnout and drugs. That's a very bad combination. Seek professional help; you are not living the life you are meant to live. We mean it!

- **Hunger and cravings**: we all get them, but are you using certain foods to help your body feel better in the short term? Look to fats, salts, and sugars. If you are using foods high in these contents you might be experiencing burnout but making your body feel safe and warm by giving it abnormally large doses of what it naturally craves.

- **Sleep**: sleep too much or too little due to anxiety or depression. Significant changes in sleep patterns or reliance on over-the-counter drugs to experience normal sleep may be indicators of serious problems.

- **Pains**: if you are having aches and pains in your body that are hard to explain, such as persistent headaches or backaches, this can be your body telling you that it is reaching a breakpoint.

If you are experiencing one or more of these symptoms examine your life to find the root cause. It may be necessary to seek medical treatment, but oftentimes something as simple as a vacation and conscious attitude adjustment will resolve the issue. Since many members of your team may crave more challenging assignments, delegating effectively may be one of those "two birds; one stone" things that really helps.

Dojo Wisdom:

> Corkboard it. The metaphor of a corkboard, a public acknowledgement of others' works, is a great thing to do. When somebody takes the time to do something, whether it is building ships in a bottle or working at the local teen center, they have chosen to spend their life energy doing something that brings them satisfaction. It is important as a leader to acknowledge positive activities that are outside your influence. This makes your team members' lives bigger. It acknowledges their value, what they choose to do with their lives, and makes a statement that you as a leader have taken initiative to shine a spotlight on them and their work. Oftentimes this is done during a staff meeting or via an organizational website or newsletter.

Action:

Sincere, meaningful, adaptable, relevant, and timely recognition is motivational, but more importantly it's the right thing to do. The challenge is that leaders who have not developed a mindset of continuously looking for opportunities to recognize others tend to get caught up in concerns of the day and never get around to doing it. Or, they assume that folks know how they feel hence never bother to say or do anything. Don't get caught in that trap. Look at other leaders who excel at recognition to find examples that you can emulate. Also consider books like *Love 'Em or Lose 'Em: Getting Good People to Stay* by Beverly Kaye and Sharon Jordan-Evans, *Make Their Day: Employee Recognition That Works* by Cindy Ventrice, or *365 Ways to Motivate and Reward Your Employees Every Day: With Little or No Money* by Dianna Podmoroff for inspiration. Morale is important and recognition is a vital aspect of building and maintaining it.

Honing the Blade:

> The things we dislike in others are oftentimes the very things we have within ourselves. Find out if that is true. If it is, take action to fix that trait immediately.

26. More Than Just Techniques

Assuring Strategic Alignment

Policy:

> *"If words of command are not clear and distinct,*
> *if orders are not thoroughly understood, then*
> *the general is to blame. But, if orders are*
> *clear and the soldiers nevertheless disobey,*
> *then it is the fault of their officers."*

Sun Tzu

Application:

> *"Tell them what you are going to tell them, tell*
> *them, and then tell them what you told them."*

Paul White

When the ancient masters developed their art forms, they lived during a time period where they not only had to fend for themselves, but during which just about any injury suffered at the hands of an adversary would mean that the victim would become incapacitated and risk death by infection or starvation. Consequently, what they invented that has survived to modern times worked very well. Those forms of training were clearly brutal and effective, but are simply not suitable for the modern citizen today.

Soldiers, law enforcement officers, and bodyguards train far more than they fight, as do martial artists. In movies and on TV we might glory at long, drawn out battles with artfully choreographed movements, but real-life altercations lasting more than a few seconds simply do not happen in predatory violence situations where people are doing their level best to hurt or kill each other. In fact, 15 to 20 seconds is unusually long. To give this a better perspective let's do a little math: Each day is made up of 86,400 seconds, so a 15 second fight takes up 0.00017 percent of your day. Fifteen seconds is an intense seventeen thousandths of a day to be sure, but it is still an infinitesimal amount of time. To average that over the amount of your lifetime, well the number would be so ridiculously small that we are not even going to calculate it.

You get the point, right? We train way, way, way more than we fight. The challenge with training is that in order to be able to put it into application we must understand more than mere techniques. That means that we need to know strategy. Every martial system contains both a strategy, which may be hidden, as well as tactics that can readily be found in the style's forms or applications. Strategy is a plan of action. In martial arts as in war, it is what you do to prepare for engagement with an enemy long before the fight begins. Tactics, on the other hand, are expedient means of achieving an end, in this case defeating an adversary. In other words, tactics are the applications that you see (or decipher), while strategy is the overarching plan that ties them together into a cohesive whole.

Looking at how frequently techniques come up in the various core forms of a classical martial system can be a good way to ascertain its strategy. Look for patterns that are repeated within and between the various *kata* (forms). Tactics are selected during the heat of battle, yet without strategy they will ultimately fail. The tactics of every combat art were developed within a strategic framework that allows them to work effectively. Everything from stances to breathing, including movement, striking, kicking, grappling, and defensive postures, are all directly tied to a system's strategy. It is holistic, self-contained, and unique to every art.

Sports teams work in much the same way, as do businesses. Any successful organization must have a sound strategy backed up by a set of viable tactics that can assure implementation. Training those tactics while keeping their strategic foundation in mind is a recipe for success. Like ripples from a pebble tossed into a pond, decisions you make can have far reaching collateral blights or benefits. Strategic thinkers are aware of potential consequences or implications of judgments they make. It is vital to rise up above the daily minutia and keep your organization or team's strategy firmly in mind as you implement plans, projects, tactics and techniques.

So, how does this work in real life? Rather than using a martial arts example we'll take a quick look at Starbucks. Their mission is "To inspire and nurture the human spirit— one person, one cup and one neighborhood at a time," which offers deep insight into their corporate strategy. The term "inspire and nurture" is largely about market segmentation. Rather than simply selling beverages, they strive to deliver an experience, one that has customers gladly paying $5.00 or more for what would otherwise be a fifty-cent cup of coffee. This strategy plays throughout the vision and principles the company instills upon its employees:

- **Our coffee**: it has always been, and will always be, about quality. We're passionate about ethically sourcing the finest coffee beans, roasting them with great care, and improving the lives of people who grow them. We care deeply about all of this; our work is never done.

- **Our partners**: we're called partners, because it's not just a job, it's our passion. Together, we embrace diversity to create a place where each of us can be ourselves. We always treat each other with respect and dignity. And we hold each other to that standard.

- **Our customers**: when we are fully engaged, we connect with, laugh with, and uplift the lives of our customers—even if just for a few moments. Sure, it starts with the promise of a perfectly made beverage, but our work goes far beyond that. It's really about human connection.

- **Our stores**: when our customers feel this sense of belonging, our stores become a haven, a break from the worries outside, a place where you can meet with friends. It's about enjoyment at the speed of life—sometimes slow and savored, sometimes faster. Always full of humanity.

- **Our neighborhood**: every store is part of a community, and we take our responsibility to be good neighbors seriously. We want to be invited in wherever we do business. We can be a force for positive action—bringing together our partners, customers, and the community to contribute every day. Now we see that our responsibility—and our potential for good—is even larger. The world is looking to Starbucks to set the new standard, yet again. We will lead.

- **Our shareholders**: we know that as we deliver in each of these areas, we enjoy the kind of success that rewards our shareholders. We are fully accountable to get each of these elements right so that Starbucks—and everyone it touches—can endure and thrive.

Powerful words, huh? Starbucks' corporate strategy of delivering an experience rather than just a product shines through, particularly in phrases like, "It's our passion," "We uplift the lives of our customers," "Our stores become a haven," "Feel this sense of belonging," and "Enjoyment at the speed of life." This is the classic customer intimacy model made real. Even in overseas locations, this customer experience is largely the same. American tourists feel right at home, yet so do the locals who have bought in to the Starbucks culture. The layout of the stores, branding, merchandising, customer interactions, and so on all play a role in fulfilling the strategy of delivering an experience rather than a product or service. What they sell, what they do, what they are, all the tactics are tied to that overarching strategy.

Can you say that your organization is as well aligned? If not, what are you going to do about it?

Dojo Wisdom:

> A strategy is a long-term plan of action designed to achieve a particular goal. Tactics, on the other hand, are expedient means of achieving an end. Like a house without a solid foundation, tactics without strategy will ultimately fail. Even as Starbucks' strategy ripples throughout their entire infrastructure, so too should your team or organization's strategy be aligned to assure that you can achieve your goals.

Action:

If you lead a team or are part of one, examine the linkage between your organization's mission and vision and your individual goals and objectives. Like the implementation of the Starbucks' business plan, there should be clear ties between the strategic goals and tactical action plans. Everyone in your group should easily be able to identify how they support the enterprise. There should be an obvious linkage clarifying how every project or task you work on a daily basis supports the higher-level priorities, products, and services delivered. If you cannot find one start asking questions. It may be time for a change.

Honing the Blade:

Strategic thinking has been a vital aspect of leadership since ancient times. In fact, the word strategy comes from the Greek word *strategos,* a title reserved for military commanders in the Athenian army.

27. Stages of Mastery

Three Phases of Your Progression as an Instructor

"A black belt, even a first-degree black belt, must possess more than technical proficiency. He must also possess a maturity greatly exceeding his skill. A black belt must also have an understanding of the principles employed in his art and be able to pass that knowledge, skill, leadership, and maturity on to others in a precise, clear, and systemic manner. All these things are what makes a 'black belt,' a black belt."

Bob Orlando

Learning martial arts is hard, yet teaching a martial art is even harder because you not only have to understand the context, strategy, applications, and techniques, but also be able to explain them to others in a way that will reach your audience. A compounding challenge is that not only do different people learn at different rates and process information differently, but also many of your students will have incongruent learning style preferences. This means that at any given point in time some folks will be deeply engaged in the learning process while others will be struggling and you'll need to find creative ways of moving things along effectively without losing anyone.

New teachers pass through three relatively distinct developmental phases as they figure out the best ways to do all that. These stages include (1) induction, (2) consolidation, and (3) mastery. It's a natural progression, but also a very long process. For example, studies show that educators in the US public school system typically take about a year to make it through the first stage, and that's when working full time. The second may take as many as five to eight years to achieve and the final stage might run another ten (or more) to reach, depending on the individual. Here's how the progression works:

1. **Induction**: during the induction period, teachers begin to understand how to assess student personalities and style predilections, how to match teaching styles with lesson plans, and how to develop content to most effectively deliver essential components of their curriculum. They learn the basics of motivating and providing feedback to students along with classroom management and discipline. It is an awkward time where theory meets reality and new teachers must realistically assess their own strengths and weaknesses in order to grow. Mentoring can expedite the process.

2. **Consolidation**: in consolidation, teachers refine their understanding to deliver developmentally appropriate lessons, more effectively tailoring materials to individual students' needs. Observational skills are sharpened and the "Plan–Do–Check–Act" cycle requires less conscious effort. Switching between teaching styles also becomes an instinctive process, enhancing class flow and content delivery. It is a time of progress where weaknesses are shored-up, and strengths are enhanced.

3. **Mastery**: mastery is evolutionary and may take a lifetime to achieve. On the journey toward mastery, teachers learn through experience and hard work to develop lessons that are enjoyable and beneficial, effective and satisfying for all involved. Delivery seems effortless as most challenges have been encountered and overcome many times before.

Dojo Wisdom:

> In a well-managed *dojo*, students are actively engaged in instructor-led activities or self-directed practice at all times. Not only do they know what they are expected to do, but they are generally successful at doing it, making progress daily, and learning something new no matter how small at each training session.

Action:

While the old adage, "those who can't do, teach" is not entirely true, the reverse often enough is. Sadly, those who "can do" often cannot teach effectively, in part because they don't know how. You see, there is both an art and a science to educating others and in the same manner that you acquired the skills you intend to teach it is only through dedication, hard work, and perseverance that can expect to become any good at it. Don't take your role as a *sensei* for granted just because you're really good at punching, kicking, grappling, and the like. Dedicate just as much effort toward mastering martial arts instruction as you did to mastering your martial art.

Write down the competencies that you expect students to master at each level of their rank progression. Using this list, identify lesson plans that will help assure they will get there as consistently and efficiently as possible. While individual students' interests and abilities often differ, there should be general uniformity in their performance at each belt level. Whenever possible invite other instructors to observe your promotion tests and provide feedback on how well you have prepared your students to perform. In this manner you can identify and correct any flaws in your instructional methodology and become a better teacher faster. Both you and your students will be better for it.

Honing the Blade:

> Sometimes we forget how much control we actually have on the world around us, falling into habit simply because, "That's the way it's always been done." We might not be able to control all the bureaucracy that is levied upon us, but we absolutely can control what we force others to endure. Think about the policies, processes, and promulgations you make from your students' point of view, identify where there's room for improvement, and take action today.

28. Doing the Right Thing

Ethics and Morals to Live and Be Remembered By

"Leadership is solving problems. The day soldiers stop bringing you their problems is the day you have stopped leading them. They have either lost confidence that you can help or concluded you do not care. Either case is a failure of leadership."

Colin Powell

Leaders must do the right thing even when the choices are very difficult, even when there is no good or right option from which to select. If you are a science fiction fan, you have undoubtedly heard of the *Kobayashi Maru*. For those unfamiliar, it was a no-win scenario given as a character test to prospective officers in the fictional Star Trek universe. The set-up was a mission to rescue a civilian vessel, the *Kobayashi Maru,* which was stranded in the neutral zone between the militant Klingon Empire (the bad guys) and Federation (the good guys) space. The approaching cadet crew had to decide whether to attempt a rescue, endangering their ship and potentially sparking an interstellar war, or leave the civilian vessel to its fate (near certain destruction).

The hero, James T. Kirk, hacks into the computer and reprograms the scenario so that he can rescue the stranded ship without getting himself and his crew killed in the process. Sometimes you can "cheat" like Kirk, using creativity or innovation to find a good way out of a "no-win" situation, but more often than not that simply isn't the case. That's when truly tough decisions must be made. What you choose will often be impactful both personally and professionally for you and everyone around you.

Think of recent headline-making scandals like the Takata airbag recall, the Veteran's Affairs Administration waiting list outrage, or the Volkswagen diesel emissions debacle. In the heat of the moment, it can be hard to do the right thing, which is why leaders must draw ethical boundaries for themselves; codes of behavior that chart their moral compasses. And, they must do it long before anything goes awry. Roughly 2,500 years ago, Greek philosopher Heraclitus of Ephesus wrote words that still resonate today:

> *"The soul is dyed the color of its thoughts. Think only on those things that are in line with your principles and can bear the full light of day. The content of your character is your choice. Day by day, what you choose, what you think, and what you do is who you become. Your integrity is your destiny... it is the light that guides your way."*

Integrity is sometimes defined as doing the right thing even when no one is watching. Without integrity it is virtually impossible to be a leader, but when things go sideways and you find yourself embroiled in scandal personal integrity is not enough. How you tackle the aftermath is often more important the problem itself. It can make or break your organization and your reputation. Consider these six things to give yourself a chance for success:

1. **Give more than others expect**: the example you set is what others will emulate. When you set the

right tone, put in the hard work, and communicate effectively, doing the right thing can become pervasive throughout the organization. Just like star players have a habit of arriving early and staying late, so do successful coaches, teachers, and businesspeople.

2. **Expect more from others**: setting high expectations for yourself and others is always important, but never more so than when it comes to ethics and culture. This must include the reward structure as well. If unscrupulous people can enhance their career, prestige, or earning potential by doing the wrong things that is exactly what most of them will do.

3. **Consider public opinion**: think about how the situation might look if it were on the front page of *The Wall Street Journal,* and then do the right thing in the eyes of the public. This gets back to Heraclitus's admonishment about bearing the "full light of day." Understand and respond to stakeholders' perceptions and expectations for you and your organization.

4. **Own the problem**: few things frustrate stakeholders more than obfuscation. You've probably heard the terms "weasel-wording" or "lawyering up." That is a really good way to lose friends and discourage people. Step up and do what is necessary to make things right. Done properly, the goodwill you generate can far exceed the cost. For example, studies consistently demonstrate that consumers would rather spend their hard-earned money at establishments that act in a socially responsible way as opposed to buying from ones that do not.

5. **Take action**: talking is not enough; issues are managed with communication but resolved through actions. No one will believe you if they do not see concrete accomplishments and corrective actions. In fact, the way you handle a problem will oftentimes be remembered far longer than the crisis itself. We all know that any cover-up is perceived as far worse than the crime.

6. **Contain quickly**: this is a crisis-communication principle. If something looks like it is out of control and has the potential of going viral (e.g., the Sandusky pedophile scandal at Penn State) it is vital to anticipate and get ahead of events. Doing the right thing alone may not be enough if you are generating headline news. In fact, if it gets to that point you will likely need to hire a professional to help you navigate the damage control process.

It can be tough to do the right thing for several reasons. To begin, you need sufficient understanding of the situation and moral clarity to figure out what "right" means in the first place. Beyond that, you need the fortitude to make tough decisions even when they may personally impact you and those you care about. Nevertheless, that's exactly what leaders do.

Dojo Wisdom:

> Most people have a pretty good moral compass. Consequently, once you understand a situation knowing the right thing is easy. While doing the right thing can be hard, it tends to get easier when you consider how your actions might look from an outsider's perspective. If you wouldn't mind seeing your story on the front page of *The Wall Street Journal* or some other prestigious national periodical, you're probably on the right track.

Action:

In the 1984 movie *Starman,* Jeff Bridges plays a human-looking alien who has come to earth. He learns to blend in by emulating other people's actions. After observing how people drive, he comes to the conclusion that, "Red means stop, green means go, yellow means go faster." It's funny in the movies, but makes an important point about real life as well. Laws are nothing more than ideas put on paper if people don't follow them.

Most folks have committed violations for speeding, jaywalking, and littering, amongst a host of other "small" things that didn't seem all that important at the time. Are you one of them? If so, would you do the same thing if your child was watching? What about if you were on a reality TV show with a national audience?

Look back to your personal mission statement. If you have not created one, now is the time. If you already have, give it a read through and make sure that you have adequately addressed the ethics and morals you wish to live and be remembered by. Circumstances can overwhelm if you do not keep those principles firmly in mind.

Honing the Blade:

> Perception oftentimes trumps reality. Facts and data alone make little difference if others are not convinced. Consequently, you not only have to model the right behaviors consistently, but also help people see the change you are making. And, be patient. The process takes time.

29. Martial Art, Martial Science

A Perspective on Owning the Path

*"There will be little rubs and disappointments
everywhere, and we are all apt to expect too much.
If one scheme of happiness fails, human nature
turns to another; if the first calculation is wrong, we
make a second better. We find comfort somewhere."*

Jane Austen

The Buddha once said, "All life is disappointment." Actually, he didn't, but as a martial arts instructor it's all too easy to see the world through that filter. You see, you are a teacher but what you are teaching is not just martial mechanics. In most instances it's also an art. And, therein lies the magic word, "art." Art is subjective, and because of its very subjectivity it brings an enormous amount of diversity into the world. Art is flexible and can be made of virtually any medium.

To a mechanical engineer there are immutable laws of nature that must be adhered to. Tab A neatly fits into slot B. Drive pylons deep into the ground to shore-up the foundation of a skyscraper for instance; don't build on sand, silt, or artificial fill. Done and done... Art, on the other hand, is an entirely different beast. While brilliant architects like Frank Lloyd Wright and Buckminster Fuller had to obey the same laws of physics as the mechanical engineer, they nevertheless created extraordinary works of art through their designs. A friend of ours owns a house designed by Frank Lloyd Wright and it's one of the coolest things we've ever seen. While it has walls, windows, and a roof like any other dwelling there isn't a single right angle in the place yet somehow it works and works well.

There is a rumor, and it need not be true for you to see the point, that one of Swiss artist Paul Klee's paintings was hung upside down at a museum of modern art for quite some time until the error was pointed out and corrected. Art can survive such things, but a similar error in architecture, or in combat for that matter, is deadly.

So, you have practiced your art, put in the hours. You sweat the sweat, spent the money, and have come to a path. Notice we didn't say conclusions, we said path. A path has boundaries and direction. Like a house without right angles, art may not have a path. Nevertheless, as a martial arts instructor you have developed a very specific method and architecture that you believe in and wish to pass along to your students. Its tradition and it is being or has been tested by others as well as by yourself. It works. But, is it the right way, the only way? To you, perhaps, but not to everyone…

Dojo Wisdom:

> There are a limited number of vital areas in human anatomy and a limited number of ways the body can move, so every martial art must share certain common elements. Emphasis and strategies differ, yet techniques overlap. Tai chi, for example, metaphorically boils an egg from the inside out with its predilection for internal energy whereas karate boils that egg from the outside in as it begins with an emphasis on external power. Nevertheless, practitioners of both arts able to defend themselves effectively, so either way we ultimately get the same boiled egg.

Action:

When somebody disappoints you, doesn't see things your way, or doesn't live up to your expectations it is important to understand their world. The student's decision is not yours. You can observe or comment, but must look at these moments from the perspective of a parent whose child is old enough to make powerful life choices. Whether they are good choices or poor choices, they're theirs to make. And sometimes you will be disappointed. It's something we all need to learn to live with.

Honing the Blade:

> Finding the right teacher is far more important than discovering the "perfect" martial art. Build a network of other instructors. Oftentimes prospective students are looking for something different than what you offer and vice versa. In this fashion you can collectively offer better, more tailored instruction to the folks who need it.

30. Passio

Leadership for the Right Reasons

"The reward for being the best through hard work is not about you. It's not for you, it's for others. It's not about praise and adulation. There is only one guarantee for achieving the level of 'best' for all your hard work, for the hours of toiling in the weight room, for grinding it out on the field, and for helping carry your team to victory... more hard work to stay there. The true reward of being the best through hard work isn't you being better than others; it's you being better for others."

Darin Slack

The Latin word *passio* means suffering or sacrifice. It is also the root word of passion (as in the Passion of Christ), though we are using it here without any religious affiliation. Anyone who is a parent may not recognize the term, yet they are intimately familiar with the concept whenever they put their child's interests ahead of their own. What responsible parent has not stayed up late to care for a sick child, help with homework, or offer a shoulder to cry on?

Yes, parents are familiar with the concept, but effective leaders are too. Most of us put others ahead of ourselves, often more frequently than we are willing to admit. We are willing to sacrifice our time, our resources, our emotional well-being, and in some cases even our lives for the things we care about—our country, our organization, our fraternity or sorority, our religion, our team, etc. In serving others we, without exception, find merit in ourselves, our purpose, and our relationship with the rest of humanity.

It's all in the attitude. If you're doing it solely for yourself people will know. They may not know today, they may not know tomorrow, but eventually they will come to see your stripes and it will be your undoing. Your actions will become suspect, all of them. If you do it for the betterment of the group, people will know that too. Ambition certainly has its place, few folks are so altruistic that they do not want and expect reward for all their hard work and sacrifice. We are all disappointed if we put in the effort and it does not come to fruition. Nevertheless, the underpinnings of all that hard work need to be selfless, working toward the betterment of the team, the organization, or even the betterment of mankind.

In the fifth-century BC, Lao-Tzu wrote:

> *"The highest type of ruler is one of whose existence the people are barely aware... The sage is self-effacing and scanty of words. When his task is accomplished and things have been completed, all the people say, 'we ourselves have achieved it!'"*

That is the difference between a leader and a manager. You do not have to be in charge to lead, but you do need to set a good example. If you are always looking out for the welfare of those in your sphere of responsibility, it's hard to go wrong. Here's an exercise to help... To advance along your leadership journey, you must be able to answer four questions with clarity:

1. What is your talent?

2. What makes you mad?

3. What did you love at the age of seven?

4. Where does this lead you?

Work fast, as overthinking puts you in your head and not in your heart. The heart works fast, the head... well that is a process. Work from your heart now. If you have already developed your personal mission statement this exercise should be easier. This may seem redundant, but the two drills go hand-in-glove, taking different tacks to provide greater clarity.

1. What is my talent?

You know you have a talent, likely more than one. Quickly, list them in no particular order; put whatever is top of mind first. Just go, now!

a. _____

b. _____

c. _____

2. What makes me mad?

One of the most common questions folks ask is what you like. If you enjoy doing something it often leads toward teaching, mentoring, or coaching others about it. But, this is not your first take for this exercise. You need to work in reverse order. Go to the opposite, determining what drives you crazy? What do you dislike? What agitates you? This process helps moves you away from what you dislike, driving clarity in where you need to go. List the top three things that make you mad here:

a. _____

b. _____

c. _____

3. What did I love at the age of seven?

Look back to your childhood. Specifically, focus your attention on what was important to you when you were about seven years old. That is the age when you began to grow your identity as an individual, started to separate from your parents who up until that time had been the center of everything in your life. This is the time period in which you are likely to find the igniter. Seek the activity where you lost track of time. Whatever lit your fire as a child likely carries over into adulthood, it is hardwired in most of us. Audit your childhood for your most joyful and fulfilling activities, behaviors, and things that you loved to do and list them here:

a. _____

b. _____

c. _____

4. Where does this lead me?

Now that you have the components, you can organize them in a meaningful way.

My talents are _____, _____, and
_____. I want to avoid_____,
_____, and _____, and I get lost in
the activities of _____, _____, and
_____.

Now, take some time to think about what you have just
written and then fill in the following sentence:

The juice of my life is: _____, I love doing
_____, and will avoid _____.

Now, knowing this, what does your life look like today? Are
you living a life that jives with your self-vision? If it is not,
why are you failing to leverage your talents, your desires, and
your fire? Sure, any old job can pay the bills, but if you are
going to spend half your life (or more) doing something to
earn a living it ought not to feel too much like work.

Dojo Wisdom:

> Take a moment to look back to the one person who
> found something in you that you did not know
> existed, a teacher, a mentor, an employer, or a coach.
> Look to how they were able to light your flame. They
> used their fire didn't they? Pay it forward. Don't try
> too hard to copy their methods, but do emulate their
> intent.

Action:

Between the exercise in this chapter and earlier ones in this
book you may have found aspects of your life, relationships,
or career that you wish to alter. Do not plan on making
wholesale changes instantly, but choose an action, set a goal,
and begin. As the old adage goes, "The journey of a thousand
miles begins with a single step."

Where to start? A terrific way is to kill the weak first. Choose one bad habit and simply say, "That is not who I am. People like me don't do _____, we take this action instead. I will do this now and into the future."

What is your choice? There is no timeline on this drill. Once you have successfully killed off the first bad habit or issue that has been holding you back in your leadership growth turn to the next item and go after it with knowledge of the success you just experienced. Sometimes it's easier, sometimes it's harder, but the momentum never ceases. This drill ends when they put the lid on your coffin and write your epitaph, a legacy you can be proud of.

Honing the Blade:

> As a *sensei,* teacher, or coach you do not often get to sit in the shade of the trees that have grown from the seeds you have planted. You do get to watch them flourish nevertheless.

Conclusion

*"Until you value yourself, you won't value
your time. Until you value your time,
you will not do anything with it."*

M. Scott Peck

The Guggenheim Museum in Manhattan New York was designed by Frank Lloyd Wright, the famous architect. Wright designed churches, skyscrapers, offices, and schools. His impression is so deep and wide that he has become a household name. Even though he passed away in 1959 his name and his legacy lives on.

Roughly 8,000 miles east of the Guggenheim is another architectural wonder, Angkor Wat. A religious complex in Cambodia, once Hindu and later repurposed as a Buddhist temple, Angkor Wat is larger than any other temple in the world. It was built in the 12th century by King Suryavarman II. Crafted of stone but interestingly without mortar, no single stone is bound to any other. Nevertheless, the complex still stands today. The greatest Roman engineers would have shaken their heads in amazement at the size and the method of building something that sophisticated.

We know who sponsored Angkor Wat, but who actually built it? The name of the architect has been lost to the winds of time. Is the genius of Angkor Wat based on the builder's name? No, but what has been left behind is a marvel nonetheless.

As Peck points out in the quote at the beginning of this section, value your time. Use it wisely, leave a sum behind, let it be good, and let it go into the future living on its own merits as you step out of the way. Follow this advice and you will have helped create a better world through your actions.

THANK YOU!

Thank you for your purchase! Publishing is an arduous process and it's folks like you who make our efforts worthwhile. With roughly 4 million new titles created every year, unbiased customer reviews are indispensable in helping readers identify books that are worth buying. To that end, if you found value from this work, please let other people know. Amazon reviews, social media posts, and the like are very much appreciated.

Bibliography

- Abraham, Jay. *Getting Everything You can out of All You've Got: 21 Ways you can Outthink, Outperform, and Out-Earn the Competition*. New York, NY: St. Martin's Press, 2000.

- Baron-Cohen, Simon. *The Essential Difference: Men, Women and the Extreme Male Brain*. New York, NY: Penguin Publishing, 2007.

- Blanchard, Ken PhD and Spencer Johnson, MD. *The New One Minute Manager*. New York, NY: HarperCollins, 2015.

- Block, Peter. *The Empowered Manager: Positive Political Skills at Work*. San Francisco, CA: Jossey-Bass Publishers, 1987.

- Cahill, Larry and Richard Haier, Nathan White, James Fallon, Lisa Kilpatrick, Chris Lawrence, Steven G. Potkin, and Michael T. Alkire. *Sex-Related Difference in Amygdala Activity during Emotionally Influenced Memory Storage*. University of California, Irvine, 2000.

- Carroll, Pete (with Yogi Roth). *Win Forever: Live, Work, and Play Like a Champion*. New York, NY; Penguin Publishing, 2010.

- Charan, Ram. *Action Urgency Excellence: Seizing Leadership in the Digital Economy*. Houston, TX: Electronic Data Systems Corp., 2000.

- Covey, Stephen M.R. and Rebecca R. Merrill. *The Speed of Trust: The one Thing that Changes Everything*. New York, NY: Simon & Schuster, 2008.

- Covey, Stephen R. and David K. Hatch. *Everyday Greatness: Inspiration for a Meaningful Live*. Nashville, TN: Thomas Nelson, 2006.

- Covey, Stephen R. *Principle-Centered Leadership*. New York, NY: Simon & Schuster, 1992.

- Covey, Stephen R. *The 7 Habits of Highly Effective People: Powerful Lessons in Personal Change.* New York, NY: Simon & Schuster, 1989.

- De Pree, Max. *Leadership is an Art.* East Lansing, MI: Michigan State University Press, 1987.

- Drucker, Peter F. *The Effective Executive.* New York, NY: Harper & Row, 1966.

- Dungy, Tony (with Nathan Whitaker). *Quiet Strength: The Principles, Practices, and Priorities of a Winning Life.* Winter Park, FL: Legacy LLC, 2007.

- Goffee, Rob and Gareth Jones. *Why Should Anyone Be Led by You? What it Takes to Be an Authentic Leader.* Boston, MA: Harvard Business School Press, 2006.

- Grant, Adam. *Give and Take: A Revolutionary Approach to Success.* New York, NY: Viking Press, 2013.

- Greenleaf, Robert K. *The Servant as Leader.* Westfield, IN: The Greenleaf Center for Servant Leadership, 2008.

- Holmes, Stanley. Cleaning Up Boeing. *Business Week,* March 12, 2006.

- Kane, Lawrence A. *Martial Arts Instruction: Applying Educational Theory and Communication Techniques in the Dojo.* Boston, MA: YMAA Publication Center, 2004.

- Kane, Lawrence A. and Kris Wilder. *The 87-Fold Path to Being the Best Martial Artist: 87 Social and Psychological Tips for Living beyond the Physical.* Burien, WA: Stickman Publications, 2015.

- Kaye, Beverly and Sharon Jordan-Evans. *Love 'Em or Lose 'Em: Getting Good People to Stay.* San Francisco, CA: Berrett-Koehler Publishers, 1999.

- Lewis, James P. *Working Together: 12 Principles for Achieving Excellence in Managing Projects, Teams, and Organizations.* New York, NY: McGraw-Hill, 2002.

- Lombardi, Vince Jr. *The Lombardi Rules: 26 Lessons from Vince Lombardi—The World's Greatest Coach (Mighty Mangers Series).* New York, NY: McGraw-Hill, 2003.

- Maxwell, John C. *The 21 Irrefutable Laws of Leadership: Follow Them and People Will Follow You.* Nashville, TN: Thomas Nelson, 2007.

- Maxwell, John C. *The 5 Levels of Leadership: Proven Steps to Maximize Your Potential.* New York, NY: Hachette Book Group, 2011.

- McKay, Matthew, PhD. Davis, Martha, PhD. Fanning, Patrick. *Thoughts and Feelings: Taking Control of Your Moods and Your Life.* Oakland, CA: New Harbinger Publications, Fourth Edition, 2011.

- Niednagel, Jonathan P. *Your Key to Sports Success.* Laguna Miguel, CA: Laguna Press, 1997.

- Peterson, David B. and Mary Dee Hicks. *Development First: Strategies for Self-Development.* Minneapolis, MN: Personnel Decisions International, 1995.

- Peterson, David B. and Mary Dee Hicks. *Leader as Coach: Strategies for Coaching and Developing Others.* Minneapolis, MN: Personnel Decisions International, 1996.

- Pink, Daniel H. Drive: *The Surprising Truth about What Motivates Us.* New York, NY; Penguin Publishing, 2009.

- Pollard, C. William. *The Soul of the Firm.* New York, NY: Harper Business, 1996.

- Rath, Tom and Barry Conchie. *Strengths Based Leadership: Great Leaders, Teams, and Why People Follow.* New York, NY: Gallup Press, 2008.

- Roberts, Dan. *Unleashing the Power of IT: Bringing People, Business, and Technology Together.* Hoboken, NJ: John Wiley & Sons, 2011.

- Savage, Charles M. *5th Generation Management: Integrating Enterprises through Human Networking.* San Francisco, CA: Digital Equipment Corporation, 1990.

- Scherkenbach, William W. *The Deming Route to Quality and Productivity.* Rockville, MD: Mercury Press, 1986.

- Scott, Susan. *Fierce Conversations: Achieving Success at Work and in Life, One Conversation at a Time.* New York, NY: The Berkley Publishing Group, 2002.

- Senge, Peter M. *The Fifth Discipline: The Art and Practice of the Learning Organization.* New York, NY: Currency Doubleday, 1990.

- Treacy, Michael and Fred. Customer Intimacy and Other Value Disciplines. *Harvard Business Review,* January, 1993.

- Waddington, Tad. *Lasting Contribution: How to Think, Plan, and Act to Accomplish Meaningful Work.* Evanston, IL: Agate Publishing, 2007.

- Wilder, Kris and Lawrence A. Kane. *Sensei, Mentor, Teacher, Coach: Powerful Leadership for Leaderless Times.* Burien, WA: Stickman Publications, 2014.

- Williamson, John N. *The Leader-Manager.* New York, NY: John Wiley & Sons, 1984.

- Wooden, John and Steve Jamison. *Wooden on Leadership: How to Create A Winning Organization.* New York, NY: McGraw-Hill, 2005.

About the Authors

Kris Wilder, BCC

Kris was inducted into the U.S. Martial Arts Hall of Fame in 2018. He runs the Cheney Karate Academy, a frequent destination for practitioners from around the world which also serves the local community. He has earned black belt rankings in three styles, karate, judo, and taekwondo, and often travels to conduct seminars across the United States, Canada, and Europe. His book, *The Way of Sanchin Kata,* was translated into Japanese, a rare honor for a Western karate practitioner.

A Nationally Board-Certified Life Coach and prolific author, Kris has lectured at Washington State University and Susquehanna University, and served as club advisor for the Eastern Washington University Karate Club. He spent about 15 years in the political and public affairs arena, working for campaigns from the local to national level. During this consulting career, he was periodically on staff for elected officials. His work also involved lobbying and corporate affairs. And, he was also a member of The Order of St. Francis (OSF), one of many active Apostolic Christian Orders.

Kris is the bestselling author of 25 books, including a Beverly Hills Book Award and Presidential Prize winner, a Living Now Book Award, a USA Best Book Awards winner, a National Indie Excellence Awards winner, an Independent Press Award winner, and a Next Generation Indie Book Awards winner. He has been interviewed on CNN, FOX, The Huffington Post, Thrillist, Nickelodeon, Howard Stern, and more.

Kris lives in Cheney, Washington. You can contact him directly at Kriswilder@kriswilder.com, follow him on Twitter (@kris_wilder), on Facebook (www.facebook.com/kris.wilder) or Instagram (https://www.instagram.com/thekriswilder/).

Lawrence A. Kane, COP-GOV, CSP, CSMP, CIAP

Lawrence was inducted into the Sourcing Industry Group (SIG) Sourcing Supernova Hall of Fame in 2018 for pioneering leadership in strategic sourcing, procurement, supplier innovation, and digital transformation. In 2022, Lawrence was honored with a Top DEIB Leader Walk the Walk Award for his commitment to Diversity, Equity, Inclusion, and Belonging. An Executive Certified Outsourcing Professional, Certified Sourcing Professional, Certified Supplier Management Professional, and Certified Intelligent Automation Professional, he currently works as a senior leader at a Fortune® 50 corporation where he gets to play with billions of dollars of other people's money and make really important decisions.

A martial artist, judicious use-of-force expert, and the bestselling author of 23 books, he has won numerous awards including a Living Now Book Award, an Independent Press Award, a Beverly Hills Book Award and Presidential Prize, a USA Best Book Award, two National Indie Excellence Awards, a NYC Big Book Award, and a Next Generation Indie Book Award, among other honors.

Since 1970, Lawrence has studied and taught traditional Asian martial arts, medieval European combat, and modern close-quarter weapon techniques. Working stadium security part-time for 26 years he was involved in hundreds of violent altercations, but got paid to watch football. A founding technical consultant to University of New Mexico's Institute of Traditional Martial Arts, he has also written hundreds of articles on martial arts, self-defense, countervailing force, and related topics.

He has been interviewed numerous times on podcasts (e.g., Art of Procurement, Negotiations Ninja Podcast), nationally syndicated and local radio shows (e.g., Biz Talk Radio, The Jim Bohannon Show), and television programs (e.g., Fox Morning News) as well as by reporters from Computerworld, Le Matin, Practical Taekwondo, Forbes, Traditional Karate, and Police Magazine, among other publications. He was once interviewed in English by a reporter from a Swiss newspaper for an article that was published in French, and found that oddly amusing.

Lawrence lives in Seattle, Washington. You can contact him directly at lakane@ix.netcom.com or connect with him on LinkedIn (www.linkedin.com/in/lawrenceakane).

Other Works by the Authors

Non-Fiction Books:

1. Martial Arts and Your Life (Kane/Wilder)

"This book is the bible of martial arts analytics!" — **Loren W. Christensen,** bestselling author of over 60 books including *The Life and Death of Sensei,* a Novel

Everyone likes to believe that they are extraordinary. As it turns out, in many ways martial artists genuinely are. To understand the full flavor of the martial arts experience, with all its depth and nuance, we conducted a comprehensive, worldwide study of practitioners. In absorbing our analysis, and meeting some remarkable individuals we highlight, you will gain a deeper appreciation for the allure and significance of the martial arts. Whether you are thinking about trying a martial art for the first time, or an experienced practitioner trying to up your game, this one-of-a-kind study will illuminate your path forward.

2. Musashi's Dokkodo (Kane/Wilder)

"The authors have made classic samurai wisdom accessible to the modern martial artist like never before!" – **Goran Powell,** award winning author of *Chojun and A Sudden Dawn*

Shortly before he died, Miyamoto Musashi (1584 – 1645) wrote down his final thoughts about life for his favorite student Terao Magonojō to whom *Go Rin No Sho,* his famous *Book of Five Rings,* had also been dedicated. He called this treatise *Dokkodo,* which translates as *"The Way of Walking Alone."* This treatise contains Musashi's original 21 precepts of the *Dokkodo* along with five different interpretations of each passage written from the viewpoints of a monk, a warrior, a teacher, an insurance executive, and a businessman. In this fashion you are not just reading a simple translation of Musashi's writing, you are scrutinizing his final words for deeper meaning. In them are enduring lessons for how to lead a successful and meaningful life.

3. The Musashi Field Manual (Kane/Wilder)

"The authors' reading of the Dokkodo makes the work accessible and applicable to our modern lives. You've made a smart move in getting this book. Don't let it collect dust on your bookshelf, put it into action!" – **Iain Abernethy**, British Combat Association Hall of Fame member

Shortly before he died in 1645 Miyamoto Musashi, the venerable "Sword Saint" of Japan, passed along his wisdom. He called this treatise Dokkodo, which translates as "The Way of Walking Alone." Dokkodo was a short essay, a mere 21 passages, yet both profound and lifechanging for the lucky few who were able fathom and follow it. When scrutinized it proves as extraordinary today as when Musashi first wrote it centuries ago. Musashi blazed the trail, now you have the privilege of following in the Sword Saint's footsteps. This manual aligns your heart and mind. It guides you toward insightful discernment and enduring self-improvement. As a result, you will walk away stronger and more prepared for all of life's tests.

4. 10 Rules of Karate (Wilder/Kane)

"Since losing isn't an option on or off the mat, this is an absolute must read for karateka." – **Christian Wedewardt**, Founder & Head of Karatepraxis

All ten precepts in this concise book cut to the heart of ending physical confrontations as quickly as possible with empty-hand techniques. Our definition of "ending" is to make the attack stop. There is no running after the now fleeing assailant to catch and strike him down. There is no lesson, no teaching, no therapy, no epiphany. There is only making that bad guy stop what he is doing instantly so that you and those you care about will be safe. These ten principles are style agnostic, all about ending fights immediately. They define how to best apply your skills and training in the real world. Those who work with these principles will find swiftness, clarity, and victory in so doing.

5. The Little Black Book of Violence (Kane/Wilder)

"This book will save lives!" – **Alain Burrese**, J.D., former U.S. Army 2nd Infantry Division Scout Sniper School instructor

Men commit 80% of all violent crimes and are twice as likely to become the victims of aggressive behavior. This book is primarily written for men ages 15 to 35, and contains more than mere self-defense techniques. You will learn crucial information about street survival that most martial arts instructors don't even know. Discover how to use awareness, avoidance, and de—escalation to help stave off violence, know when it's prudent to fight, and understand how to do so effectively when fighting is unavoidable.

6. Sh!t Sun Tzu Said (Kane/Wilder)

"If you had to choose one variant of Sun Tzu's collected work, this one should be at the top of the pile... I loved it!" – **Jeffrey-Peter Hauck**, MSc, JD, Police SGT (Ret.), LPI, CPT USA, Professor of Criminal Justice

Sun Tzu was a famous Chinese general whose mastery of strategy was so exceptional that he reportedly transformed 180 courtesans into skilled soldiers in a single training session. While that episode was likely exaggerated, historians agree that Sun Tzu defeated the Ch'u, Qi, and Chin states for King Ho-Lu, forging his empire. In 510 BC, Master Tzu recorded his winning strategies in Art of War, the earliest surviving and most revered tome of its kind. With methods so powerful they can conquer an adversary's spirit, you can use Master Tzu's strategies to overcome any challenge, from warfare to self-defense to business negotiations. This book starts with the classic 1910 translation of *Art of War*, adds modern and historical insight, and demonstrates how to put the master's timeless wisdom to use in your everyday life. In this fashion, the *Art of War* becomes accessible for the modern mind, simultaneously entertaining, enlightening, and practical.

7. The Big Bloody Book of Violence (Kane/Wilder)

"*Implementing even a fraction of this book's suggestions will substantially increase your overall safety.*" – **Gila Hayes**, Armed Citizens' Legal Defense Network

All throughout history ordinary people have been at risk of violence in one way or another. Abdicating personal responsibility by outsourcing your safety to others might be the easy way out, but it does little to safeguard your welfare. In this book you'll discover what dangers you face and learn proven strategies to thwart them. Self-defense is far more than fighting skills; it's a lifestyle choice, a more enlightened way of looking at and moving through the world. Learn to make sense of "senseless" violence, overcome talisman thinking, escape riots, avert terrorism, circumvent gangs, defend against home invasions, safely interact with law enforcement, and conquer seemingly impossible odds.

8. Dude, The World's Gonna Punch You in the Face (Wilder/Kane)

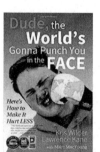

"*As an emergency room physician, I see a lot of injuries. This book can save you a lot of pain and trauma, not just physical but also emotional and financial as well. Do yourself a favor, read it, and stay out of my Emergency Room.*" – **Jeff Cooper**, MD

We only get one shot at life. And, it's really easy to screw that up because the world wants to punch us all in the face. Hard! But, what if you knew when to duck? What if you were warned about the dangers—and possibilities—ahead of time? Here is how to man-up and take on whatever the world throws at you. This powerful book arms young men with knowledge about love, wealth, education, faith, government, leadership, work, relationships, life, and violence. It won't prevent all mistakes, nothing will, but it can keep you from making the impactful ones that you'll regret the most. This book is quick knowledge, easy to read, and brutally frank, just the way the world gives it to you, except without the pain. Read on. Learn how to see the bad things coming and avoid them.

9. <u>Sensei Mentor Teacher Coach</u> (Wilder/Kane)

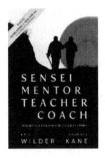

"Finally, a book that will actually move the needle in closing the leadership skills gap found in all aspects of our society." – **Dan Roberts**, CEO and President, Ouellette & Associates

Many books weave platitudes, promising the keys to success in leadership, secrets that will transform you into the great leader, the one. The fact of the matter is, however, that true leadership really isn't about you. It's about giving back, offering your best to others so that they can find the best in themselves. The methodologies in this book help you become the leader you were meant to be by bringing your goals and other peoples' needs together to create a powerful, combined vision. Learn how to access the deeper aspects of who you are, your unique qualities, and push them forward in actionable ways. Acquire this vital information and advance your leadership journey today.

10. <u>Dirty Ground</u> (Kane/Wilder)

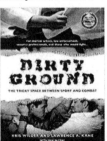

"Fills a void in martial arts training." – **Loren W. Christensen**, Martial Arts Masters Hall of Fame member

This book addresses a significant gap in most martial arts training, the tricky space that lies between sport and combat applications where you need to control a person without injuring him (or her). Techniques in this region are called "drunkle," named after the drunken uncle disrupting a family gathering. Understanding how to deal with combat, sport, and drunkle situations is vital because appropriate use of force is codified in law and actions that do not accommodate these regulations can have severe repercussions. Martial arts techniques must be adapted to best fit the situation you find yourself in. This book shows you how.

11. <u>Scaling Force</u> (Kane/Miller)

"If you're serious about learning how the application of physical force works—before, during and after the fact—I cannot recommend this book highly enough." – **Lt. Jon Lupo**, New York State Police

Conflict and violence cover a broad range of behaviors, from intimidation to murder, and require an equally broad range of responses. A kind word will not resolve all situations, nor will wristlocks, punches, or even a gun. This book introduces the full range of options, from skillfully doing nothing to employing deadly force. You will understand the limits of each type of force, when specific levels may be appropriate, the circumstances under which you may have to apply them, and the potential costs, legally and personally, of your decision. If you do not know how to succeed at all six levels covered in this book there are situations in which you will have no appropriate options. More often than not, that will end badly.

12. <u>Surviving Armed Assaults</u> (Kane)

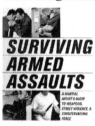

"This book will be an invaluable resource for anyone walking the warrior's path, and anyone who is interested in this vital topic." – **Lt. Col. Dave Grossman**, Director, Warrior Science Group

A sad fact is that weapon-wielding thugs victimize 1,773,000 citizens every year in the United States alone. Even martial artists are not immune from this deadly threat. Consequently, self-defense training that does not consider the very real possibility of an armed attack is dangerously incomplete. You should be both mentally and physically prepared to deal with an unprovoked armed assault at any time. Preparation must be comprehensive enough to account for the plethora of pointy objects, blunt instruments, explosive devices, and deadly projectiles that someday could be used against you. This extensive book teaches proven survival skills that can keep you safe.

13. The 87—Fold Path to Being the Best Martial Artist (Kane/Wilder)

"The 87—Fold Path contains unexpected, concise blows to the head and heart... you don't have a chance, but to examine and retool your way of life."
– **George Rohrer**, Executive and Purpose Coach, MBA, CPCC, PCC

Despite the fact that raw materials in feudal Japan were mediocre at best, bladesmiths used innovative techniques to forge some of the finest swords imaginable for their samurai overlords. The process of heating and folding the metal removed impurities, while shaping and strengthening the blades to perfection. The end result was strong yet supple, beautiful and deadly. As martial artists we utilize a similar process, forging our bodies through hard work, perseverance, and repetition. Knowing how to fight is important, clearly, yet if you do not find something larger than base violence attached your efforts it becomes unsustainable. *The 87-Fold Path* provides ideas for taking your training beyond the physical that are uniquely tailored for the elite martial artist.

14. How to Win a Fight (Kane/Wilder)

"It is the ultimate course in self-defense and will help you survive and get through just about any violent situation or attack." – **Jeff Rivera**, bestselling author

More than 3,000,000 Americans are involved in a violent physical encounter every year. Develop the fortitude to walk away when you can and prevail when you must. Defense begins by scanning your environment, recognizing hazards and escape routes, and using verbal de-escalation to defuse tense situations. If a fight is unavoidable, the authors offer clear guidance for being the victor, along with advice on legal implications, including how to handle a police interview after the altercation.

15. Lessons from the Dojo Floor (Wilder)

"Helps each reader, from white belt to black belt, look at and understand why he or she trains." – **Michael E. Odell**, Isshin-Ryu Northwest Okinawa Karate Association

In the vein of Dave Lowry, a thought-provoking collection of short vignettes that entertains while it educates. Packed with straightforward, easy, and quick to read sections that range from profound to insightful to just plain amusing, anyone with an affinity for martial arts can benefit from this material. This book educates, entertains, and ultimately challenges every martial artist from beginner to black belt.

16. Martial Arts Instruction (Kane)

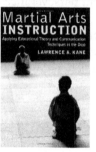

"Boeing trains hundreds of security officers, Kane's ideas will help us be more effective." – **Gregory A. Gwash**, Chief Security Officer, The Boeing Company

While the old adage, "those who can't do, teach," is not entirely true, all too often "those who can do" cannot teach effectively. This book is unique in that it offers a holistic approach to teaching martial arts; incorporating elements of educational theory and communication techniques typically overlooked in *budo* (warrior arts). Teachers will improve their abilities to motivate, educate, and retain students, while students interested in the martial arts will develop a better understanding of what instructional method best suits their needs.

17. The Way of Kata (Kane/Wilder)

"This superb book is essential reading for all those who wish to understand the highly effective techniques, concepts, and strategies that the kata were created to record." – **Iain Abernethy**, British Combat Association Hall of Fame member

The ancient masters developed *kata*, or "formal exercises," as fault—tolerant methods to preserve their unique, combat-proven fighting systems.

Unfortunately, they also deployed a two-track system of instruction where only the select inner circle that had gained a master's trust and respect would be taught the powerful hidden applications of *kata*. The theory of deciphering *kata* was once a great mystery revealed only to trusted disciples of the ancient masters in order to protect the secrets of their systems. Even today, while the basic movements of *kata* are widely known, the principles and rules for understanding *kata* applications are largely unknown. This groundbreaking book unveils these methods, not only teaching you how to analyze your *kata* to understand what it is trying to tell you, but also helping you to utilize your fighting techniques more effectively.

18. The Way of Martial Arts for Kids (Wilder)

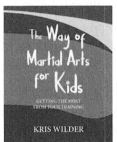

"Written in a personable, engaging style that will appeal to kids and adults alike." – **Laura Weller**, Guitarist, *The Green Pajamas*

Based on centuries of traditions, martial arts training can be a positive experience for kids. The book helps you and yours get the most out of every class. It shows how just about any child can become one of those few exemplary learners who excel in the training hall as well as in life. Written to children, it is also for parents as well. After all, while the martial arts instructor knows his art, no one knows his/her child better than the parent. Together you can help your child achieve just about anything... The advice provided is straightforward, easy to understand, and written with a child-reader in mind so that it can either be studied by the child and/or read together with the parent to assure solid results.

19. The Way of Sanchin Kata (Wilder)

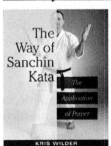

"This book has been sorely needed for generations!" – **Philip Starr**, National Chairman, Yiliquan Martial Arts Association

When karate was first developed in Okinawa it was about using technique and extraordinary power to end a fight instantly. These old ways of generating remarkable power are still accessible, but they are purposefully hidden in *sanchin kata* for the truly dedicated to find. This book takes the practitioner to new depths of practice by breaking down the form piece-by-piece, body part by body part, so that the very foundation of the *kata* is revealed. Every chapter, concept, and application is accompanied by a "Test It" section, designed for you to explore and verify the *kata* for yourself. *Sanchin kata* really comes alive when you feel the thrill of having those hidden teachings speak to you across the ages through your body. Simply put, once you read this book and test what you have learned, your karate will never be the same.

20. Journey: The Martial Artist's Notebook (Kane/Wilder)

"Students who take notes progress faster and enjoy a deeper understanding than those who don't. Period." – **Loren W. Christensen**, Martial Arts Masters Hall of Fame inductee

As martial arts students progress through the lower ranks it is extraordinarily useful for them to keep a record of what they have learned. The mere process of writing things down facilitates deeper understanding. This concept is so successful, in fact, that many schools require advanced students to complete a thesis or research project concurrent with testing for black belt rank, advancing the knowledge base of the organization while simultaneously clarifying and adding depth to each practitioner's understanding of his or her art. Just as Bruce Lee's notes and essays became *Tao of Jeet Kune Do*, perhaps someday your training journal will be published for the masses, but first and foremost this notebook is by you, for you. This is where the deeper journey on your martial path toward mastery begins.

21. The Way to Black Belt (Kane/Wilder)

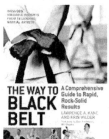

"It is so good I wish I had written it myself." – **Hanshi Patrick McCarthy**, Director, International Ryukyu Karate Research Society

Cut to the very core of what it means to be successful in the martial arts. Earning a black belt can be the most rewarding experience of a lifetime, but getting there takes considerable planning. Whether your interests are in the classical styles of Asia or in today's Mixed Martial Arts (MMA), this book prepares you to meet every challenge. Whatever your age, whatever your gender, you will benefit from the wisdom of master martial artists around the globe, including Iain Abernethy, Dan Anderson, Loren Christensen, Jeff Cooper, Wim Demeere, Aaron Fields, Rory Miller, Martina Sprague, Phillip Starr, and many more, who share more than 300 years of combined training experience. Benefit from their guidance during your development into a first-class black belt.

22. Wolves in Street Clothing (Wilder/ Hollingsworth)

"Teaches folks to rekindle tools that are already in us—already in our DNA—and have been there for thousands of years." – **Ron Jarvis**, Tracker, Outdoorsman, Self-Defense Instructor

This book gives you a new light in which to see human predatory behavior. As we move farther and farther from our roots insulating ourselves in technology and air-conditioned homes we get disconnected from the inherent and innate aspects of understanding the precursors to violent behavior. Violence is not always emotionally bound, often and in the animal kingdom is simply a tool to access a needed resource—or to protect an essential resource. Distance, encroachment, and signals are keys to avoiding a predator. Why would a cougar attack a man after a bike ride? Why would a bear attack a man in a hot tub? Why would a thug rob one person and not another? The predatory animal mind holds many of the keys to the answer to these questions. Learn drills that will help you tune your focus and move through life safer and more aware of your surroundings.

23. 70-Second Sensei (Kane/Wilder)

"I'll let you in on a secret. The 70-Second Sensei is a gateway drug. It's short, easy to read, and useful. It has stuff in it that will make you a better instructor. Even a better person." — **Rory Miller**, Chiron Training

Once you have mastered the physical aspects of your martial art, it is time to take it to the next level— to lead, to teach, to leave a legacy. This innovative book shows you how. Sensei is a Japanese word, commonly translated as "teacher," which literally means "one who has come before." This term is usually applied to martial arts instructors, yet it can signify anyone who has blazed a trail for others to follow. It applies to all those who have acquired valuable knowledge, skills, and experience and are willing to share their expertise with others while continuing to grow themselves. After all, setting an example that others wish to emulate is the very essence of leadership. Clearly you cannot magically become an exemplary martial arts instructor in a mere 70-seconds any more than a businessperson can transform his or her leadership style from spending 60-seconds perusing The One Minute Manager. You can, however, devote a few minutes a day to honing your craft. It is about giving back, offering your best to others so that they can find the best in themselves. And, with appreciation, they can pay it forward...

24. The Contract Professional's Playbook (Nyden/Kane)

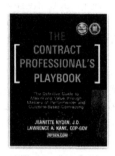

"*While early career practitioners may understand the value of drafting, negotiating, and managing exceptional contracts, they often struggle to master the requisite skills. This comprehensive manual helps structure the negotiation process, thereby minimizing the perilous process of trial-and-error, expediting competency with leading practices and tools that can help reduce risk and speed outcomes for both buy-side and sell-side alike.*" — **Gregg Kirchhoefer**, P.C., IAOP Leadership Hall of Fame Member

Ever increasing demand for performance- and outcome-based agreements stems from pressure for enterprises to drive greater value from their strategic customer/supplier relationships. To achieve expected performance, contractual relationships are increasingly complex and interdependent, requiring more stakeholders be involved in the decision making. Unfortunately for contract professionals held accountable to these requirements there has been little in the way of resources that answer their "how to" questions about drafting, negotiating, and managing performance- and outcome-based agreements. Until now! *The Contract Professional's Playbook* (and corresponding eLearning program) walks subject matter experts who may be new to complex contracting step-by-step through all aspects of the contract life cycle. Invaluable competencies include identifying and managing risk, increasing influence with stakeholders, developing pricing models, negotiating complex deals, and governing customer-supplier relationships to avoid value leakage in the midst of constant change. It's an invaluable resource that raises the bar for buy-side and sell-side practitioners alike.

24. There are Angels in My Head! (Wilder)

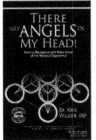

"This is not a book on doctrine, dogma or collection of creeds to memorize in order to impress others with knowledge. This is a practical application of your participation in a new experience. Here you will find your questions answered even before they are asked."
– **Br. Rich Atkinson**, Order of St. Francis

The unexplainable has happened. A prayer has been answered, a gift has been given, a communication has occurred... Is it the voice of God, or the voices in your head? Here's how to find out: In this groundbreaking book, you will discover the organization of the mystical experience. Based on the classic works of G. B Scaramelli, an 18th Century Jesuit Priest, Wilder brings modern relevance to any person to apply to their journey as they seek the Divine. Using examples and principles from Christianity and other religions, Wilder demonstrates that mankind's profound mystical experience crosses all cultures and religions.

Fiction Books:

1. Blinded by the Night (Kane)

"Kane's expertise in matters of mayhem shines throughout." – **Steve Perry**, bestselling author

Richard Hayes is a Seattle cop. After 25 years on the force, he thinks he knows everything there is to know about predators. Rapists, murderers, gang bangers, and child molesters are just another day at the office, yet commonplace criminals become the least of his problems when he goes hunting for a serial killer and runs into a real monster. The creature not only attacks him, but merely gets pissed off when he shoots it. In the head. Twice! Surviving that fight is only the beginning. Richard discovers that the vampire he destroyed was the ruler of an eldritch realm he never dreamed existed. By some archaic rule, having defeated the monster's sovereign in battle, Richard becomes their new king. When it comes to human predators, Richard is a seasoned veteran, yet with paranormal ones he is but a rookie. He must navigate a web of intrigue and survive long enough to discover how a regular guy can tangle with supernatural creatures and prevail.

2. <u>Legends of the Masters</u> (Kane/Wilder)

"It is a series of (very) short stories teaching life lessons. I'm going to bring it out when my nephews are over at family dinners for good discussion starters. A fun read!" – **Angela Palmore**

Storytelling is an ancient form of communication that still resonates today. An engaging story told and retold shares a meaningful message that can be passed down through the generations. Take fables such as *The Boy Who Cried Wolf* or *The Tortoise and the Hare*, who hasn't learned a thing or two from these ancient tales? This book retools Aesop's lesser-known fables, reimagining them to meet the needs and interests of modern martial artists. Reflecting upon the wisdom of yesteryear in this new light will surely bring value for practitioners of the arts today.

DVDs:

1. <u>121 Killer Appz</u> (Wilder/Kane)

"Quick and brutal, the way karate is meant to be." – **Eric Parsons**, Founder, Karate for Life Foundation

You know the *kata*, now it is time for the applications. *Gekisai (dai ni), Saifa, Seiyunchin, Seipai, Kururunfa, Suparinpei, Sanseiru, Shisochin*, and *Seisan kata* are covered. If you ever wondered what purpose a move from a *Goju Ryu* karate form was for, wonder no longer. This DVD contains no discussion, just a no-nonsense approach to one application after another. It illuminates your *kata* and stimulates deeper thought on determining your own applications from the *Goju Ryu* karate forms.

2. Sanchin Kata: Three Battles Karate Kata (Wilder)

"A cornucopia of martial arts knowledge." – **Shawn Kovacich**, endurance high—kicking world record holder (as certified by the Guinness Book of World Records)

A traditional training method for building karate power, *sanchin kata* is an ancient form. Some consider it the missing link between Chinese kung fu and Okinawan karate. This program breaks down the form piece by piece, body part by body part, so that the hidden details of the *kata* are revealed. This DVD complements the book *The Way of Sanchin Kata*, providing in-depth exploration of the form, with detailed instruction of the essential posture, linking the spine, generating power, and demonstration of the complete *kata*.

3. Scaling Force (Miller/Kane)

"Kane and Miller have been there, done that and have the t—shirt. And they're giving you their lessons learned without requiring you to pay the fee in blood they had to in order to learn them. That is priceless." – **M. Guthrie**, Federal Air Marshal

Conflict and violence cover a broad range of behaviors, from intimidation to murder, and they require an equally broad range of responses. A kind word will not resolve all situations, nor will wristlocks, punches, or even a gun. Miller and Kane explain and demonstrate the full range of options, from skillfully doing nothing to applying deadly force. You will learn to understand the limits of each type of force, when specific levels may be appropriate, the circumstances under which you may have to apply them, and the potential cost of your decision, legally and personally. If you do not know how to succeed at all six levels, there are situations in which you will have no appropriate options. That tends to end badly. This DVD complements the book *Scaling Force*.